Clairvoyance

The Ultimate Psychic Development Guide to Extrasensory Perception and Intuition

© Copyright 2021

The contents of this book may not be reproduced, duplicated or transmitted without direct written permission from the author.

Under no circumstances will any legal responsibility or blame be held against the publisher for any reparation, damages, or monetary loss due to the information herein, either directly or indirectly.

Legal Notice:

You cannot amend, distribute, sell, use, quote or paraphrase any part or the content within this book without the consent of the author.

Disclaimer Notice:

Please note the information contained within this document is for educational and entertainment purposes only. No warranties of any kind are expressed or implied. Readers acknowledge that the author is not engaging in the rendering of legal, financial, medical or professional advice. Please consult a licensed professional before attempting any techniques outlined in this book.

By reading this document, the reader agrees that under no circumstances are is the author responsible for any losses, direct or indirect, which are incurred as a result of the use of information contained within this document, including, but not limited to, errors, omissions, or inaccuracies.

Contents

INTRODUCTION 1
CHAPTER ONE: PSYCHIC ABILITY IN YOU AND THOSE AROUND YOU 3
    EMPATH 6
    MEDIUMSHIP 8
    TELEPATHY 10
    SIGNS THAT YOU HAVE PSYCHIC ABILITIES 13
CHAPTER TWO: BENEFITS OF EXTRASENSORY PERCEPTIONS 15
CHAPTER THREE: TYPES OF PSYCHICS - WHICH ONE ARE YOU? 18
    CLAIRVOYANCE (CLEAR SEEING) 19
    CLAIRAUDIENCE (CLEAR HEARING) 21
    CLAIRSENTIENCE (CLEAR FEELING) 24
    CLAIRCOGNIZANCE (CLEAR KNOWING) 26
    CLAIRALIENCE (CLEAR SMELLING) 28
    CLAIRGUSTANCE (CLEAR TASTING) 30
CHAPTER FOUR: LOCATING AND RELEASING BLOCKAGES 32
    HOW TO RELEASE AN EMOTIONAL BLOCKAGE 39
    OTHER WAYS OF RELEASING PSYCHIC BLOCKS 41
CHAPTER FIVE: ACTIVATING THE THIRD EYE AND TRUE MINDFULNESS 45

Third Eye Foods 49
　Third Eye Affirmations 51
　Meditation Techniques for the Third Eye 52
　The Trataka Technique 55
CHAPTER SIX: HOW TO INTUIT AND READ THE ENERGY OF THOSE AROUND YOU 60
CHAPTER SEVEN: GETTING TO KNOW THE CHAKRAS 70
　Root Chakra 72
　Sacral Chakra 73
　Solar Plexus Chakra 74
　Heart Chakra 76
　Throat Chakra 77
　Third Eye Chakra 78
　Crown Chakra 80
　How Chakra Balancing Impacts Psychic Development 81
　Clearing and Balancing the Chakras 84
　Balancing the Root Chakra 84
　Balancing the Sacral Chakra 85
　Balancing the Solar Plexus Chakra 86
　Balancing the Heart Chakra 87
　Balancing the Throat Chakra 88
　Balancing the Third Eye Chakra 88
　Balancing the Crown Chakra 89
CHAPTER EIGHT: READING AURAS 91
　How to See Auras 95
　Aura Colors and Their Meanings 98
CHAPTER NINE: DAILY EXERCISES AND HABITS FOR STRENGTHENING INTUITION AND PSYCHIC ABILITY 102
CONCLUSION 106
HERE'S ANOTHER BOOK BY MARI SILVA THAT YOU MIGHT LIKE 107
REFERENCES 108

Introduction

I recently met someone who could overwhelmingly feel the emotions of the people around them. This person could instantly tell when someone was experiencing a particular emotion because they felt it as if it was their own. Although they knew they had this ability, they had no idea why. They just lived each day, bombarded by stimuli from their environment. Little did they know they were what is known as an "empath." It always surprises me how many people go through life with different psychic gifts without realizing it. I have had many people contact me to ask me if they had intuitive and psychic gifts. "Am I clairvoyant? How do I know?" If you are reading this you probably also suspect you have these abilities, but you are not sure.

Everyone is psychic to an extent. We were all born with extrasensory instincts that give us these abilities, but these senses become dormant in most people because we focus on the five "normal" senses of sight, smell, touch, taste, and hearing. So, if you are wondering, then yes, you have latent psychic abilities. You may not have used them for all of your life, but they are there waiting to be awakened. With the right guide, you can awaken your inner senses and use your gift, whatever it is.

Naturally, many resources claim to teach people how to awaken and develop their psychic gifts. Many people pay self-acclaimed psychics to help them hone their special abilities. Unfortunately, most of these resources don't offer practical or helpful insight that can benefit people looking to refine their intuition and change their lives. Fortunately, Clairvoyance: The Ultimate Psychic Development to Extrasensory Perception and Intuition is the exception.

This book is your ultimate guide to psychic development, extrasensory perception, and intuition. Whether you want to see auras, read people's energy, communicate with your mind, or communicate with extraterrestrial beings, everything you want to know is here. It does not matter whether you are a beginner or looking to advance in your psychic development journey. This book has something for everyone. From the first page to the very end, it is filled with practical techniques, proper steps, and straightforward exercises to help you sharpen your intuition and learn clairvoyance. With this book, you will have a handy resource to go to anytime for guidance on your way to psychic awakening.

Chapter One: Psychic Ability in You and Those Around You

Clairvoyance is defined as the ability to see beyond what the ordinary eye can see. It is the ability to obtain knowledge unknown to other people through extrasensory perception. Clairvoyance does not happen through the usual channels of perception you know. A clairvoyant person can "see" inside your mind without you realizing it. Clairvoyant is a psychic ability. Every psychic has extrasensory perceptions not known to the majority.

Before I go on, I should note that "every psychic" in this context refers to every human. Many people believe that psychics are special people with unique gifts. This is just a misconception that became popular over the years due to a mix of different factors. Contrary to what many believe, extrasensory perception isn't exclusive to a handful of unique people. We all naturally possess that power, even though many of us may not realize it yet.

If you have someone around you that dreams of things yet to happen, such a person may be clairvoyant. You have people with these gifts around you, but you probably don't realize it. If you don't know what to look for in a person, you cannot be sure of their psychic ability. People have different psychic abilities. Some can see beyond the physical, while others can communicate with others using their mind. Some can even feel your emotions precisely as you are experiencing them. They can tell you what you are feeling at a particular moment.

Many people go to psychics to discover things about themselves. For instance, some people go to help investigate a decision they are making. They do this for reassurance or affirmation they are about to make the right decision. But what these people don't know is that they can usually do these things themselves if they are willing and ready to learn. If you awaken your extra senses like the expert psychics, you have no reason to see a psychic. You already have the ability, and it is just latent. You need to awaken your power and use it to make a difference in your life. Remembering that this book is about psychic development, we will be discussing different psychic abilities other than clairvoyance.

Often, people assume that clairvoyance and "psychic" are the same things. Like the other abilities we will discuss, clairvoyance is a psychic ability. "Psychic" is like a broad spectrum under which you have different abilities. Psychic development and experiences range from clairvoyance to telepathy, precognition to clairsentience, and many others. Let's briefly look at what "psychic" is so that you can understand what I mean.

"Psychic" was originally a Greek word, and in English, it translates to "Soul Personality Energy." This is what we refer to as spirit energy. Everyone has soul personality energy. This energy is transcendental. It goes beyond the material plane and can make us so much more than we realize. Soul personality energy encompasses the physical and spiritual realm. It embodies the entire mystical plane. Like everyone else, you have a body and soul. The five senses you use for seeing, hearing, feeling, smelling, and tasting are the sense of your physical body. Your extrasensory senses, on the other hand, are the senses of your soul. We were all raised to take care of our physical body to keep it vibrant and healthy. But only a handful of people out of the millions worldwide know to care for their souls.

Your soul is what makes you psychic. The fact that you have a soul means you are already psychic. You cannot access your psychic ability because you weren't taught to use your extra-senses like you were taught to use your other senses. Also, you were not taught to care for your spirit like you care for your physical body. Caring for your soul in a nurturing way is one key to psychic awakening. To use your abilities consciously, you only need to work out your spiritual "muscles." More important, you need to get rid of any ideas and beliefs that can hold you back from achieving psychic awakening. This is a vital step to regaining your inborn abilities.

Thanks to Hollywood, many people have a cliché expectation of what it means to be clairvoyant or have a psychic gift. In movies and shows, psychics are portrayed as receiving visits from supernatural beings such as demons and angels. Of course, it is possible to see and communicate with these beings. But it does not happen as Hollywood wants you to believe. To know whether you are clairvoyant or psychic, there are signs you can watch out for. The most common sign is the gut feeling every human has.

Have you ever thought about doing something and then decided against it, only to discover it would have had a terrible outcome for you? That is what you call a *gut feeling*. It is when you intuitively know something, even though you have no previous knowledge of that thing. When that happens, it is your psychic sense communicating to you. For example, suppose you made plans with your friends to hang out at your favorite spot after work. Unfortunately, you had to cancel with your friends because you suddenly didn't feel like going with them. Something deep inside you tells you to stay at home and just watch a new movie. The next day, your friends inform you they couldn't make it to the spot after all due to a significant road blockage. In that case, your gut feeling was right.

Besides the power of intuition and gut feelings, there are other signs to watch out for if you want to know if you are psychic. But before we get to that, I would briefly like to explain the different abilities that one can have.

Empath

An empath is a person with the psychic ability to feel the emotions of other beings intensely. They are susceptible and vulnerable to their environment. People like this experience an influx of emotions that leave them feeling very raw and vulnerable. If you are an empath, you may develop anxiety and behave erratically due to the bombardment of people's emotions. An empath can be physical, emotional, and intuitive. But based on this ability is the psychic sense of clairsentient. If your primary psychic sense is clairsentience, then you are more likely to be an empath than anything else. Soon, I will explain more about the five psychic senses.

Humans are all born with the emotion of empathy, but this emotion is heightened in clairsentient people. Noting the difference between the two is vital for an adequate understanding of psychic empathy. Unlike the raw human emotion of empathy, psychic empathy goes beyond merely feeling others' emotions. These empaths can also sense and read other people's energy. They can pick up on non-verbal and non-visual cues of what someone else is experiencing. Some psychic empaths can sense the energy vibrations from other people, how they feel their emotions. Others are claircognizant, so they simply know what you feel even if you give no clues. Suppose you can read people's energy, or you regularly feel overwhelmed by energy when you are around people. There, you are likely a psychic empath.

Like I said, empaths can be physical, emotional, or intuitive. A physical empath unconsciously responds to the emotions of those around them and the physical signs of those emotions. If you always find yourself mirroring the feelings of people you are around, you could be a physical empath. For instance, if you feel happy when you are with people expressing joy and laughing regardless of your current condition, which is a sign.

Similarly, if you experience physical discomfort whenever you are with those who are ill or experiencing similar symptoms, that is another sign. Physical empaths manifest other people's symptoms, and they barely have control over them. As a physical empath, the best way to control this is always to surround yourself with vibrant and healthy people. If you have people who generally add to your stress levels, it is best to avoid those people.

An emotional empath is who you generically call an empath. If you find yourself experiencing the happiness or pain of others as if it were yours, you could be an emotional empath. With this psychic ability, you find yourself picking up on others' positive and negative feelings. When you are around happy people, you feel thrilled. Likewise, you feel unfortunate when you are around sad people. Being around people always in crisis mode can negatively affect your mental and emotional energy. An intuitive empath is the same thing as an emotional empath, with a slight difference. Rather than feel, they sense feelings. They can sense what is unexpressed. They also can tell when someone is lying or being truthful.

How to tell if you are a psychic empath:

- You are overwhelmed by feelings whenever you are in the company of people.
- You find it challenging to maintain closeness and intimacy
- You prefer to self-isolate
- You find nature comforting
- Your senses are extra sharp
- You have a powerful gut feeling

Example: Your friends have invited you to hang out at a restaurant. You are excited and looking forward to the date. On D-day, you prepare and head for the venue. As soon as you take your first step into the building, you feel bombarded by different sensations at once. You experience a mix of different emotions at once, and you feel highly uncomfortable. The date with your friends wasn't exactly a wholesome experience because you spent most of the time getting strange feelings you knew weren't yours. After that day, you didn't go out for another three days because you felt drained and needed to recharge. This kind of thing happens to you every time you go out to a public place.

Mediumship

Like clairvoyance, mediumship is also used loosely as a synonym for psychic. But a psychic is not always a medium, even though any medium is a psychic. Whether you are a spiritual medium, intuitive medium, or psychic medium, the basis of it is that you have these abilities. Without being clairvoyant, you cannot be a medium. If you don't know who a medium is, mediums are psychics with the ability to communicate with spirits in the afterlife. Essentially, a medium can talk to ghosts and spiritual beings. Being a medium goes beyond merely using your sense of intuition to read energy, feelings, or gather information about people.

As a medium, your clairvoyance allows you to see a person's past, present, and future life by connecting and communicating with the person's spirit energy. So, mediums use non-physical energy emitting outside of themselves to get the information they need about a person. If you have a mediumship gift, you might have noticed that you often see people who have passed away in your dreams. And when they appear, they usually have information for you. Usually, mediums show signs of their ability in childhood. But they may not realize what it is until they are adults. Some don't realize or bother with it forever.

Mediumship requires you to be intuitive, which everyone is. So, anybody can also be a medium if we train our inner senses. While you may not be able to communicate with every spirit, you can certainly communicate with your loved ones who have passed away. Spirits are all around you, and they are willing to communicate with you if you have the skill to sense, feel, or hear them. Depending on your most prominent clairvoyance sense, you can either see spirits, hear them, feel them, or just know their presence. Mindfulness is key to becoming a medium because you always must know everything around you. If you are mindful, you will find that most things that appear strange, odd, or coincidental to you are signs from your loved one.

How do you know if you are a medium?

You often receive sensations that remind you of a dead loved one. For example, you may receive a whiff of their favorite perfume when they were alive or taste their favorite food in your mouth out of nowhere.

- You have vivid dreams about them regularly.
- Sometimes, you just know things in your mind, and you feel like that information is from them.
- You always have the feeling that someone is around you and trying to communicate with you.
- You experience Déjà vu.

Example: Your grandmother just passed away. You were close to her when she was alive, so her death was excruciatingly painful for you. After the funeral, you to go clean her house. Suddenly, you have an intuitive thought about her basement and feel like you must go down there. So, you go down to her basement. Once there, you look around. Voila, you find a box that contains your grandma's most valued bracelet. The box also has a note stating that your grandma left you the bracelet to remember her by. This is an instance of mediumship.

Even though you may not realize it at that moment, your grandmother's spirit put the thought about the basement in your head. If you improve your skills, you will communicate with your grandmother whenever you need her guidance. It is common for dead loved ones to serve as spirit guides for their family members.

Telepathy

When you think of communication, the first thing that naturally comes to mind is verbal and written communication; that is writing and speaking. But have you ever thought about the possibility of communicating through the mind? Without a doubt, you have heard of telepathy before. Chances are that your perception of telepathy is what you watch in your favorite superhero shows. Hollywood has a penchant for making movies about superheroes with mystical power. But the reality is that you don't have to be Charles Xavier to communicate with people through the mind. If you are psychic, you already possess the gift of telepathy. It is a natural gift we all possess as humans. From the beginning of time, humans have had the inborn ability to connect with others through the mind.

To define telepathy, it is a psychic gift that allows you to send or receive thoughts and feelings from other people, regardless of distance. Like all psychic abilities, telepathy is a form of extrasensory perception. You don't need your physical senses to send and receive messages telepathically. Telepathy can take place in different forms. First, is reading or the ability to sense or hear what is in another person's mind. Next, there is communicating - direct mental communication with another individual. Then, you must impress –the ability to plant a word, a thought, or an image in someone else's mind. Finally, there is control - the ability to compel another person to think or behave in a specific way.

As a human, you have the natural ability to know things and feel them as they are. That is how you form your experiences. You also can link your consciousness with that of other people. It all concerns your soul personality energy, which allows you to align your vibrational frequency with another person. When you achieve that, you don't need your normal physical senses to communicate or connect with the person. Whether you know it or not, you have likely had different instances of telepathic experiences. If you have ever had an experience where your gut feelings told you something was amiss with someone and you then find that to be true, then you have had a telepathic experience.

As you can see, one thing common with all these psychic abilities is intuition. Suppose you learn to align yourself with the vibrational frequencies of others consciously. There, you can form a mental connection with them.

How do you know that you are telepathic?

- The space between your eyebrows constantly aches and tingles. You also experience other sensations that make you uncomfortable.

- You are naturally empathetic. Telepathy and empathy are interrelated. While empathy has more to do with accessing others' feelings, telepathy is more related to thoughts. Also, while an empath receives information about others' feelings, a telepath can transmit and receive. If you have the gift of empathy, you can train yourself to open your telepathic doorway for further psychic development.

- You feel drawn to the spirit world. People who are subconsciously self-aware of their psychic gifts often find themselves pulled towards psychic and spiritual practices. Suppose you feel the pull to connect with your ancestors, meditate, or generally spend time doing spiritual activities. There, which means your gift is waiting to be awakened.

- You can tell when someone is lying to you or deceiving you. People with the gift of telepathy can sense when someone isn't straightforward or accurate with them. If they haven't yet realized their gifts, they subconsciously pick up on the other person's thoughts. But when they become conscious of their potential and work on honing the skill, they can do this consciously.

Example: Your boyfriend is going to school in another state. Even though he has been gone for six months, you communicate with him every night. It is almost like a ritual between you. One day, you get a strong feeling in your gut that something isn't right. You are worried something might have happened to him. That feeling in your gut persists throughout the day. You can't get him off your mind. As soon as night comes, you call his line, and he tells you he had a minor accident and is in the hospital. He says it is nothing serious, and he will be released the next day. You are relieved, but you think back to the uneasy feeling in your gut.

This is an example of a telepathic experience between two partners who share powerful feelings for each other. Telepathic experiences can happen between parents and children, siblings, lovers, and twins. Twin telepathy is a prevalent type of telepathy between twins.

These are some of the most known psychic abilities that use extrasensory perception. Others include precognition, astral travel, lucid dreaming, etc. One thing common with these abilities is that they are all founded on the gift of clairvoyance. You are probably wondering how to tell you if you have psychic gifts. The signs you get the most will determine the exact psychic ability you have.

Signs That You Have Psychic Abilities

There are signs all around you that show you have extrasensory perception. Still, you are probably not paying attention to those signs. To be sure that you have clairvoyant psychic abilities, below are signs to look out for. Note that you don't have to see all these signs to be clairvoyant. If you experience at least three of these signs, you are clairvoyant.

- **Strong Gut Feelings:** If you find that your gut feelings are usually accurate, this is one of the best and most common signs to watch out for. Everyone generally has gut feelings, but they are often more substantial when there is a psychic pull. When there is a psychic pull, you feel like you are being directed toward something by a strong force, and you have that sense of knowing. Besides, normal gut feelings occur occasionally. But when you have a psychic pull, you get that sense of knowing most the time.

- **Extra Sharp Senses:** Being psychic means you have extrasensory perception. If you feel like your sense are sharper than usual, that is another sign. You may hear things that are not there. You may find you can sense the thoughts and feelings of another person. A great example is if you always complete other people's sentences before they even say them out. Suppose this always happens to you with different people at different times. There, you may can communicate with others telepathically.

- **Vivid Dreams:** If you often have dreams that feel so real to the extent that they don't go away for hours, this could be another sign of extrasensory perception. For example, if you had a dream about a job you applied for but got rejected, you may receive a call from the organization the next day. Vivid dreams don't happen just at night. You can also have daydreams. For instance, you may daydream about a trophy being awarded to you, only to discover that you've been offered a promotion at work. Always pay attention to your dreams because they can tell you about your psychic abilities.

• **Drawn to Nature and Beautiful Things**: Psychics are usually drawn to nature and other beautiful things. If you like visiting the beach or hanging out in the woods at the back of your home, this could also be another sign. Psychics find they are drawn to nature and aesthetics more often than others. Clairvoyance makes you appreciate things such as painting, drawing, photography, and other creative activities. This is because clairvoyance is a visual sense.

• **See Auras**: As a clairvoyant, it is common to see colored lights around everyone you encounter. The light you see is called the aura, the human electromagnetic field's visual projection. Auras give you vital information about people and their thoughts and feelings. They can help you understand yourself and the world better.

The next chapter focuses on the benefits of psychic gifts and why you should develop yours.

Chapter Two: Benefits of Extrasensory Perceptions

Like all things, extrasensory perceptions have advantages and perks. It is impossible to argue or deny the benefits that psychic gifts give to those aware of them. Naturally, being psychic comes with responsibilities that one must live up to. You must be cautious of your psychic abilities and how you use them. One mistake can affect you in ways you don't yet know. Possessing extrasensory perceptions is a fascinating thing. It allows you to view the world from a unique perspective. With this unique perspective, you can make vital decisions and put yourself on the right path toward fulfilling your purpose. More importantly, you can also help others with your ability.

One benefit of being psychic is that it allows you to tune in with all that is while raising your vibration. Using your psychic gift is one way to raise your vibration. The more you use your ability, the more you can connect with the universe and everything within it. As I have noted, everything in the universe comprises energy. You are made of energy. I am made of energy. Every being in the universe is energy. It exists within us all and connects us in a fascinating way. When you hone and use your psychic ability, your ability to tune in with the energy of the universe dramatically improves. Eventually, you can even connect with your higher self, which is the goal of all spiritual people. Connecting with your higher self gives you access to guidance from the divine and other spiritual beings higher than you.

Also, using your psychic abilities requires you to meditate. Without meditation, you cannot reach the higher vibrational state that allows you to use your gifts consciously. Also, you need to use your psychic gifts to keep your chakras opened and aligned. Chakras are a part of the energy system. To maintain a healthy physical, mental, and spiritual life, you need to ensure that your chakras are always clear, balanced, and healthy.

If you are a beginner to clairvoyance and psychic development, chances are that your chakras are blocked. This means that your physical and spiritual health may not be as vibrant as they should be. To unblock and align your chakras, you need first to start your psychic awakening and development journey. Aside from this, your chakras are directly connected with each of your psychic senses. This means that using your psychic gifts and keeping your chakras balanced and open enhances your psychic abilities.

Also, being psychic allows you to explore your spirituality and the spiritual realm. To start psychic development, you first need to learn to meditate correctly. When you meditate, you are propelled into places that your physical body cannot ordinarily access. This provides an opportunity for you to learn more about yourself. For example, you can access the place of Akashic Records using your psychic abilities. The Akashic Records contain information about your past life, your present, and your future. By accessing the records, you can learn more about the things that will affect your life. While exploring the spiritual realms, you can communicate with angels, spirit guides, deities, and other spiritual beings that could impact your life with their knowledge.

Your psychic gifts can help you understand your direction in life, and your life purpose. Clairvoyance gives you invaluable insight into the complexities that life has for you. Even if you are, by default, a highly organized person, it is easy to become overwhelmed due to the number of decisions you must make throughout your lifetime. But if you are in tune with your psychic senses, these decisions need not be hard to make. You have access to Divine guidance on your life and its purpose. Essentially, you can always get a unique, spiritual overview when you need it. This will prevent you from overthinking and over-analyzing your choices before you make vital life decisions.

Just as psychic abilities have perks, they also have risks. If you are not cautious, you could end up using your gifts for selfish reasons. If this happens, you could lose your access to that aspect of yourself. Exploitation is not something you should use your abilities for. Also, be careful not to use the information you get through your powers for wrongful deeds. Remember that the future is continually changing as it is based on possibilities. So, you should take none of your predictions as the absolute truth. Finally, be careful not to overuse your abilities, which can cause a strain on your mental and physical health. If you allow yourself to become so immersed in the spiritual world, you may lose your touch with reality. There should be a balance between your exploration of the physical plane and the spiritual plane.

To achieve psychic growth, those are a few things to remember. By keeping these tips in mind, you can maximize the benefits of your abilities while minimizing the risks.

Chapter Three: Types of Psychics - Which One Are You?

If someone asked you what psychic abilities are, you probably wouldn't know what to tell them. It is hard to clearly describe what a psychic is. The main difference between types of psychics is their ability to perceive information. Your prominent psychic sense defines your psychic ability. Therefore, it determines the type of psychic you are.

The psychic senses also refer to what psychic abilities you have. Of course, you already know that being psychic or clairvoyant means you can perceive things beyond your mainstream senses. But what exactly do you know about psychic abilities? Are all psychics the same, or are they different? If different, what are the types called "The Clair Senses." Everyone is born with one or more of these senses, but we often lose touch with them. Each of these senses works differently for every individual, but information received through them generally comes in abstract ways. Sometimes, you may even need other tools to decipher the messages you receive. For example, if you want to tell your friend to come over to your house later, there are multiple ways of doing that. You could call them on their cell phone, send them a text message, send a voice note on WhatsApp, or shout out to them if they live next door. These are ways to communicate one message to your friend, but they are different channels. This means that they all deliver the same message differently. The same goes for psychic senses and communication.

With each psychic sense, you can get the same message, but in different ways. Clairvoyance brings messages to you in the form of visuals. But clairsentience allows you to "feel" instead of seeing. When you start tuning into your psychic senses, you may not know which is which. You may not even realize when using these senses. Because they all work with intuition, it's challenging to know your prominent "clair" sense. As you get to know the senses, you may realize that you have all these abilities or one or two of them. It does not matter whether you have one or more. What matters is that you are psychic, whether you have just one of these senses or more.

So, the question is, how do you recognize the "clair" senses?

Clairvoyance (Clear Seeing)

Clairvoyance is the number one psychic sense known to most people. It is the first thing that comes to mind when you ask someone if they know what a psychic is. As a result, most people often assume that clairvoyance is the same thing as being a psychic. Clairvoyance means "clear seeing," which, in other words, means psychic seeing. Put simply, clairvoyance is the ability to see psychic messages. It is safe to say that clairvoyance is usually the most active sense in most people. Regardless of your age or gender, you have most likely experienced clairvoyance before in one way or another. The exciting thing is that you may have experienced it more than once without recognizing it for what it is. Due to clairvoyance being the most common psychic sense, many dismiss it as wishful thinking, daydreaming, and the wandering of the mind. This misunderstanding stems from the misrepresentation in movies and TV shows.

The best way you can think of clairvoyance is to imagine a visual playing in your head, but every clairvoyant psychic has different views on what they see. Some receive messages in the form of a mobile screen that suddenly appears in their head with pictures, symbols, etc. Others depict visuals of people and objects with distinctive features. When clairvoyants see spirits, they often materialize so it is incredibly real. If you experience this, you may feel as though you were looking at a real person in front of you. But really, you are using your "mind's eye" rather than your physical eye. So, they are not really in front of you; you can't touch them. But you can see them in your mind.

In movies, clairvoyance is depicted as something that plays out in the mind of the psychic, although clairvoyants usually get images and symbols to interpret to get the full message or answer. If you are a clairvoyant psychic, you more than likely receive messages in subtle ways, so you need to know what to look for. Otherwise, you may convince yourself that your mind is just making things up.

If your psychic type is clairvoyant, you may:

- Receive random mental images
- Imagine or visualize things easily
- See color, images, symbols, etc. in flashes
- Have visions in the form of a movie in your head

Visualization is a huge part of clairvoyance due to it being clear seeing. If clairvoyance is your prominent psychic sense, it would be nothing for you to imagine yourself tanning on a beach in Hawaii. This means that daydreams come easily to you.

Some ways you receive clairvoyant messages are:

- **Symbols**: As stated earlier, symbols are one way that clairvoyant messages are received. It applies to other psychic abilities. Most of the time, psychic messages come in symbols. Initially, you may be confused about the meaning of the symbol. Still, you can interpret it if you cultivate your intuitive gift. For example, instead of being shown directly that you are getting a promotion at work, you may see images of a trophy on your shelf. You shouldn't worry if you don't understand the symbols right away. The more you practice and work with your spirit guides, the better you will decipher symbols. If you receive the messages, interpreting the meanings won't be a problem for you.

• **Images and Videos**: As you have learned, clairvoyants don't receive messages in the same way. We don't always see the same things. So, while you receive yours as symbols, someone else may be receiving images and movies. This image could come as a snapshot in the mind. It could also come in the form of moving images, like when watching a slideshow. For some, it could be a symbol in the form of an image.

The common denominator in the different ways clairvoyant psychics receive messages is that they all come through the Third Eye. Clairvoyant messages aren't physically visible. You need your psychic sight to see them, which is the eye in the located center of your forehead. Your third eye is also what you call the mind's eye. It is the channel through which clairvoyant psychics receive messages. The Third Eye will be discussed in detail in Chapter Five.

Clairaudience (Clear Hearing)

Clairaudience is the gift of psychic hearing. It is the inborn ability to "hear" messages without using your physical ears. Just as clairvoyance is about seeing, clairaudience is about hearing. This means you receive messages in the form of sounds rather than images or symbols. A clairaudient person may hear ideas, instructions, or messages in their head suddenly. The voice you hear will be similar to your voice tone, so it differs from hearing voices. It may feel like you are talking to yourself, not like someone else is talking to you. The voice you hear can be internal or external. Internal means you hear the voice within yourself, while external means that the voice or noise comes outside of yourself.

Clairaudient messages usually sound like a pronounced thought. It is soft and subtle, so some people assume they are thinking out loud. Clairaudience is key to telepathic communication. Understandably, you may find it hard to understand clairaudient messages since spirits usually have to lower their vibration before they can communicate with you. This causes their voices to become jerky. Voices are not the only thing you hear as a clairaudient psychic.

Messages also come as music or sounds. Mediums are clairaudient. They hear words, names, phrases, and messages from the voices of those who have passed on. Sometimes, clairaudient messages are received as physical sounds from the ethereal plane. This is one of the rare occasions where the voice comes to you externally. When this happens, you hear the sound, music, or words using your physical voice - yet you cannot identify a source of the voice. Sometimes, the voice of the spirit sending you the message sounds like their voice rather than your own.

Clairaudient messages may also be in the form of warnings. Let's say you are in distress, and your spirit guide wants to help you get out of that situation. There, you may hear a loud warning in your head. This could be a startling experience for you, but it shouldn't be scary. One reason spirits prefer to send their messages in subtle forms is to avoid scaring you. Initially, you may not understand where the messages are coming from or why you are receiving them in your psychic development journey. Clairaudient messages could be from your spirit guide, a loved one who has passed away, or your Higher Self.

Everybody can decipher hearing to some extent, but some people are more predisposed to it because it is their prominent psychic sense. To tell if clairaudience is your dominant sense, check out these signs below.

- You are musically inclined. You like listening to music and playing musical instruments.

- You love to connect to your inner self by writing your own music.

- Auditory channels are your preferred ways of learning. This means you would rather listen to someone explain something to you than read about that thing yourself.

- Noise makes you feel irritable and sensitive.

- Most of the time, you hear ringing and high-pitched sounds in your head.

- You are inclined to thinking and spending a lot of time in your head.

It is normal if you don't have all the traits listed above, but you need to have at least three to confirm if clairaudience is your dominant psychic ability. If you don't, it is still possible that you are clairaudient to some extent. Also, here is a list of how to identify when you have a clairaudient experience.

- You hear voices that sound like your own.

- You often hear the voices internally, but they also come from an external source occasionally.

- The experiences are short and straight to the point.

A friend once told me about a clairaudient experience he had that saved his life even though he didn't realize what it was. He was going somewhere with his friends. They were all in one car. Suddenly, he heard a voice in his head that told them all to fasten their seatbelts firmly. He was surprised because he couldn't identify the source of the voice.

But he told his friends what the voice in his head had said. They all laughed and put on their seatbelts, anyway. Some moments later, they felt their car get hit from behind by another vehicle, which was much bigger. Fortunately, they were not injured because they had all worn their seat belts. My friend still narrates the story to anyone who cares to listen. He often talks about how a "strange voice" saved his life and that of his friends.

Clairsentience (Clear Feeling)

This is the dominant psychic sense in empaths and highly sensitive people. Clairsentience is the ability to sense or receive messages via emotions, feelings, and physical sensations. For instance, say changes are being made at your place of work. These changes mean that some people will be laid off or sent to a remote branch. Naturally, everyone feels frustrated and tense about the situation, but it is worse for you. You are stressed and anxious. You feel drained, but you have no idea why. You feel like you are going crazy because you don't know why you are reacting to the changes much worse than your coworkers are.

In a scenario like this, the chances you are clairsentient are high. Although you don't know it, you are soaking up the emotions that everyone else in your workplace is feeling. Now imagine all those emotions from several people going through the mind of one person simultaneously. You are bound to feel drained, exhausted, and overwhelmed.

Clairsentient psychics can pick up on every feeling, emotion, sensation, and energy around them regardless of how subtle these things are. They often need to take alone time to recharge after spending time with people. Such people find it hard to watch the news or watch tragic movies because they feel the characters' emotions more intensely than ordinary people. Fortunately, clairsentience is one of the lesser-known psychic abilities, so it has not been widely misrepresented in movies.

A clairsentient receives intuitive messages through sensing. If you typically feel a way about people, places, or objects, you could be a clairsentient psychic. Being clairsentient means knowing what someone feels before they even utter a word about it to you. A typical clairsentient might feel pangs of hunger deep in their stomach when they pass by homeless people. Or they may become sad after watching tragic news on the TV.

If your psychic type is clairsentient, you have likely had a clairsentient experience and just didn't realize what it was. For instance, you may know that you become way too sad when you watch tragic movies, but you have no idea why you feel this way. Here are a few things that clairsentient psychics experience.

- Feel emotional or physical pain from other people
- Have accurate instinctual feelings about people, places, objects, or situations
- Find it hard to function well in crowds due to an overwhelming influx of feelings
- Get drained when around people
- Feel drained due to watching the news

If you get called emotional by your friends, you are probably a clairsentient psychic. The good thing about clairsentience is that once you learn of it, you can train yourself to become less susceptible to the feelings and energies of people around you.

Clairsentient psychic ability may not sound as glamorous as other types that involve seeing or hearing spirits, but it has its benefits. As you develop your clairsentience more, you will find you can use this gift to help other people. You can also use it to receive spiritual guidance from above.

Claircognizance (Clear Knowing)

Do you often complete people's sentences midway? Are your instincts always accurate? If you find yourself "just knowing" things, claircognizance is likely to be your psychic type or one of your dominant senses. Claircognizance is the ability of psychic knowing. It is the fourth of the major psychic abilities. This is an ability that allows you to know something without a logical explanation to back it up. Claircognizance results from powerful gut feelings. Intuitions are often stronger in claircognizant psychics than they are in other senses. When a claircognizant gets a gut feeling, it is often so strong that they can't dismiss it even if they want to.

As a claircognizant, you "know" things without an explanation for how you know them. It is like thoughts and ideas just pop up into your head. The thing about claircognizant messages is that they are usually specific. When you think of claircoginzance, imagine information, ideas, and facts that appear in your awareness or perception about other people and circumstances. This information often seems like inspired ideas when they pop up in your head. For example, you just know that you can't trust a person, and you end up being right. Or, you get a sense of knowing about a job vacancy, and you apply for the job. Usually, claircognizant psychic messages appear in your head like an illuminating bulb that suddenly lights up and goes off in the blink of an eye. They are usually random, and they can happen at any time, whether you are working, watching a movie, eating, or sometimes, doing something unrelated to the message.

The line between regular thoughts and claircognizant messages can be blurry, meaning you may find it difficult to tell them apart. The human mind has repetitive thoughts invested in protecting us. It is easy to mistake claircognizant messages for this kind of thought, but they are distinctive from each other. To know whether your thoughts are just thoughts or claircognizant messages, here are six signs that can help you make the distinction.

- **Accurate Instincts:** As humans, we all have instincts geared toward ensuring our survival. These instincts are formed and developed from our upbringing, experiences, and sometimes, genetic makeup. But they sometimes turn out to be wrong. This is the opposite of claircognizance. As a claircognizant psychic, your instincts are always accurate. You can predict an event yet to happen simply based on your gut feelings because that is how strong the accuracy is. Claircognizance means you just know when not to accept that offer, go to that party, or trust that person trying to make a business deal with you. You don't know why, but you just know.

- **Detect Lies:** Claircognizant psychics are the practical definition of a human lie detector. If you always know when someone is dishonest with you, it may be a sign you have the gift of claircognizance. Remember that this is common with some other psychic senses, so you must compare it with the other signs before determining whether you are claircognizant. Having the gift of claircognizance means you always know when someone is lying or being insincere with you. Nothing gets past you. Because of this, people will trust your submissions or suggestions about others easily.

- **Random Ideas and Solutions**: Let's say you have a problem you are trying to solve. You have been working on the problem for hours, but you can't seem to solve it. Suddenly, an idea pops into your head about the solution. Quickly, you apply this idea, and it turns out to be right. If the scenario described has occurred to you once or twice, you might be claircognizant. If random ideas and suggestions often appear in your head to help you solve a problem or make a decision this is a clear sign. Claircognizant psychics receive messages in the form of thoughts, ideas, or suggestions that come to them. The exciting thing is these messages can come at any time of the day. You may randomly get a message while watching the latest episode of your favorite TV series or even when you are working out. When these ideas randomly pop up, the best thing you can do is observe them and try to interpret whatever they mean. Since claircognizance works closely with gut feelings, you most likely will always know what the message is about. Usually, claircognizant messages tend to be specific.

Tuning in with your claircognizance sense is one of the best ways to awaken or to develop your psychic abilities. It honestly makes everything so much easier for you. So, always pay attention to your guts and use that to connect with your clear sense of knowing.

Clairalience (Clear Smelling)

One of the most powerful senses in both the physical and spiritual realms is the sense of smell. It can evoke emotions and memories in such an incredible way. Whether it is the scent of a freshly cut lawn or your grandmother's favorite soup, certain scents have a more profound level of meaning to you. Clairalience is the psychic sense of smell that often occurs to most people, whether they are in tune with their psychic side or not. It often happens as a sort of guidance or sign from your spirit team. Although it is not as common or known as previously thought, clairalience is a beautiful ability that can benefit you in many ways.

Clairalient individuals often find they can sniff out and smell things imperceptible to others. Often, the scents or smells contain divine messages or information from the psychic realm. You can tell if you have this gift by the way different smells affect your mood. Do you find that some smells are pleasant to you while others are repugnant? If you pay attention to the surrounding scents, you probably will find hidden meanings. You can determine if you have claralience by observing how you feel before, during, and after specific smells. If you repeatedly get a particular smell from around you, it could be your spirit guide, or a dead loved one trying to pass you information.

A typical example of claralience is when you repeatedly smell your dead grandfather's favorite cologne days after he was buried. When you keep getting a scent that reminds you of a loved one who has passed away, it is a possible sign that that person's spirit is around you. It could also mean that their spirit is trying to communicate something to you. There, you need to be patient and try to interpret whatever they are trying to communicate. The smell can be anything from their favorite cookie to their favorite tobacco brand. It was something dear to them while they were alive. The right thing is to acknowledge whenever you experience something like this. Acknowledge their presence and try communicating with them. Or you can recall your favorite memories of them. The experience may be short or long, but the point is to take advantage of that moment to let them know that you feel their presence. They will appreciate that simple gesture from you.

Sometimes, your angels will communicate with you through clairalience. If claralience is your dominant psychic ability, your angel may send a smell when they are around you. The smell is likely to be a subtle and sweet flowery scent. When you notice a smell like this that has no physical source, it is a pointer to a higher dimensional being. Paying attention to all the odors you come across every day is key to training yourself. When you develop this gift, you can use it to achieve a range of things.

First, you can use claralience to access memories that are otherwise difficult to recall. A simple smell can bring back a surge of memories about a person or a circumstance that you have nearly forgotten on your conscious level. It can be something as simple as smelling your partner's favorite perfume and immediately feeling their presence. It can also be as complicated as smelling something that triggers a repressed childhood memory.

Smells also allow you to read people. You can quickly form a psychic impression of someone through their smell. You can tell when they are dishonest by using their smell to get a reading on them. No matter how subtle an odor is, you can use it to know whether they are uncomfortable, ill, scared, lying, or on the other another, have a crush on you. You can literally "smell" their emotions and thoughts.

Clairalience allows you to sense energy. Sometimes, you go to another person's space and immediately realize that you are not comfortable in that space. At first, you may not know why you feel that way. But if you tune into your psychic sense of smell, you can get a lot of information about the space and why you feel uncomfortable being there. Clairalience makes you capable of "smelling" danger, literally. Just like you smell food and can instantly tell if it is rotten or good to eat, you can use your clairalience sense to smell danger. Even if you cannot define what you sense at that moment, trust your sense that something isn't right.

Everyone, including you, emanate a natural scent that originates from their energy vibrations. Even if claralience isn't your dominant ability, you can pick up on this smell from everything around you with energy. But if you are clairalient, you can pick up on scents much stronger than the ordinary ones. Using this ability, you can alter people's moods by aligning your natural scent with theirs. It is a powerful gift you can use to impact the mood of people who need comfort and support from you.

Clairgustance (Clear Tasting)

Clairgustance is the extrasensory perception of taste. Every time you put a food item or object in your mouth, you subconsciously taste the energy and flavor. But clairgustance goes beyond this. It focuses more on the sensations of specific taste you receive in your mouth even when you have nothing in your mouth. If clairgustance is your dominant psychic ability, it means you can potentially taste the energies of every energetic thing in the universe. This means you regularly receive random tastes in your mouth. Often, the tastes you receive are connected to someone you know or an experience you had. For example, if you receive the taste of the one soup your late grandmother used to make for you the most while she was alive, that is a clear sign of clairgustance. Like claralience, this psychic ability is your spirit team's way of communicating with you.

To determine the message and figure out the meaning, you need to do some detective work on your part. Pay attention to the taste you get – do you randomly get the taste in your mouth at a specific time of the day? What or who does the taste remind you of? The possibilities and interpretations are endless, but you will decipher the meaning if you put in the work. Sometimes, the taste can add a layer of meaning to a broader context in alignment with another psychic sense.

No matter your psychic type, you can tap in and enhance your senses with practice and patience. It does not matter whether you are a beginner just starting or someone that already has a bit of knowledge about psychic abilities. If you have more than one of the psychic senses, lucky you. But even if you have only one dominant sense, you can train yourself to develop all psychic senses. You naturally have all these senses. Even if clairvoyance is your dominant ability, you can develop the other clair senses just as much as your clairvoyant ability. This goes for all other abilities.

Chapter Four: Locating and Releasing Blockages

Starting your psychic awakening is always an interesting process. You gain interest in spirituality, go through self-discovery, and work on developing your intuitive and psychic abilities. Naturally, you are excited because you can't wait to use your gifts. You are in the honeymoon phase of the psychic development process. You are sure that you are already building a strong connection with your psychic senses. There is nothing more exciting than this, but suddenly, you find you can't receive intuitive hits. No matter how much you practice and meditate, you see nothing that makes you feel like all your hard work and dedication are paying off. Eventually, you lose interest in becoming psychic. You think to yourself, "What is the point? It doesn't work after all."

The above is a succinct description of most people when they start developing their psychic abilities. The initial stage can be exciting. But when you get to where you feel like you should have received psychic hits, it may not be as exciting to you as it once was. When many people find themselves in this situation, their first conclusion is that psychic gifts are not real, but they are as real as the moon, the sun, and other fantastic creations of nature that are all around us. The problem is these people can't access their gifts due to psychic and energy blockages. Before you find yourself in this same situation where you can't keep the faith because you don't know the basis of things, you should learn all about blockages. More importantly, know why they obstruct your access to your psychic gifts and how you can get rid of them.

To help you understand what a psychic block is, I need to remind you what psychic abilities entail. At the beginning of this book, I categorically stated that psychic abilities originate from our soul's personality energy. You may have a human body, but foremost, you are a soul in a physical body having human experiences. By default, you were created as a high vibrational being. This makes you psychically open to your environment. Your connection is stronger when you are a child due to your open-mindedness, purity, and innocence, but as you grow older, you begin to lose your psychic connection to the universe through negative reprogramming and destructive societal expectations. Think of an instance where you have a new house with new windowpanes that are as clear as daylight. Without use, the windowpanes accumulate dust, and eventually, it loses a clear view.

Metaphorically, the dust in this context is what you may call a psychic blockage. These blockages make it difficult or nearly impossible for you to access your intuitive and spiritual gifts. Unless you find and release the blockage, you may never access your psychic senses or use them for anything. Many people aren't even conscious of their psychic gifts because the blockages prevent them from having the most basic psychic experience.

Different things can cause blockages, but emotions are some of the most common reasons. In some people, a blockage is caused by physical reasons. Your emotions can disrupt the natural flow of energy through your system, and they play a vital role in your experiences and life. Positive emotions typically improve the flow of energy by increasing energy levels. They include feelings of joy, happiness, excitement, empathy, compassion, hope, etc. Positive emotions are also known to attract people with similar positive energy. Negative emotions such as fear, anger, worry, hatred, and anxiety, drain you of your will.

At one point in your life, you must have suppressed your emotions. We all generally have developed the ability to suppress our childhood emotions due to several factors. We don't realize that emotional suppression can hinder our ability to access our psychic abilities. Your emotions were made to be expressed, not suppressed. They need an outlet. When you suppress or repress your emotions, your body stores the emotion away, and it becomes a blockage. Unless you release the blockage, it can manifest in physical symptoms of anxiety, pain, migraine, chronic pain, etc. More importantly, it blocks your access to your gifts.

Contrary to what was described at the beginning of this chapter, some people start their training well. They get intuitive hits, and then suddenly, the hits stop, and they can't access their psychic sense anymore. Here, you may be wondering what went wrong. Your answer goes back to the windowpane analogy I gave earlier. You are born with unobstructed access to your spirit or soul. Then, you start acquiring beliefs, ideas, and opinions that make you doubtful of your gifts' possibilities. Also, you encounter negative people and have negative experiences. This is when the dust starts covering up your view.

When you start with the spiritual discovery and start your psychic awakening, you are cleaning the dust from the windowpane. The more you train, the clearer the window (your spirituality) becomes. So, if you keep cleaning and then you stop mid-way, what happens? The window accumulates dust again. This same thing goes for psychic blocks. Suppose you practice, but you are not consistent with it. There, there is no way you can break through the obstruction between you and your spiritual connection with the energy of the universe.

You are not perfect; nobody is. The world isn't perfect either. It's quite normal that you are subconsciously forming opinions about these things every day as you meet people, interact with them, and encounter different situations. You sometimes have these opinions consciously. Some encounters you have can make you experience low vibration emotions, including anger, fear, doubt, stress, suspicion, judgment, and other feelings. Spirit cannot align with the low vibration emotions because it operates at a higher vibrational level. So, it aligns with emotions such as love, joy, happiness, and faith. These are higher vibrational feelings.

There are different types of blocks. The place where the block is determines what the block is called. Some blocks are visible, meaning they are easy to find. Others are not so visible, meaning they can be affecting your life while you can't locate them due to their obscurity. Below, here are ten types of psychic blockages and where you can locate them in your system. After we discuss how to locate the blockages, we will then move on to how you can release them and gain access to your psychic senses.

Auric Blockage

Psychic blocks occur in the auric field due to a distortion of energy. Blocks within the auric layers occur frequently in many people. The blocks usually occur because of internal energy slowing down and becoming stuck. They also occur due to external negative energies infiltrating your aura. Examples are imprints and attachments such as implants or etheric cords. When there is a blockage in the aura, it may appear like symptoms related to the energy that caused the blockage or the place where the blockage is located. One of the best ways to get rid of blocks in the auric field is to clean the aura, repair it, remove attachments, and attune the frequency. More importantly, you also need to maintain the aura to keep it healthy.

Chakra Blockage

The chakras are part of the energy compositions that make up your energy field and bodies. Energy flows into your energy bodies and out to your physical body through the chakras. There are seven chakras in the system, and each chakra has different symptoms which represent an energy blockage. When there is a blockage in any of the chakras, it affects the entire chakra system. But it doesn't stop there. It also affects your physical and mental health. A blocked chakra disturbs your whole system's functioning because it restricts your ability to emit and bring in energy. This, in turn, lowers your vibration and makes it impossible to align with your spirit. To release any blockage in the chakras, you need to clear, open, align, and balance your chakras. Once your chakras are open and balanced, they will maintain their healthy states.

Emotional Blockage

Emotional blockage happens in several subtle energy bodies at once, making them more complicated than most types of blockages. But the primary location is usually the emotional layer of the auric field. When there is a blockage in the emotional body, it inadvertently affects the chakras, especially the Sacral Chakra and the meridians. The auric layers extend to one another, meaning that energy needs to go through some to reach others. If one layer is blocked, there will be no way to circulate energy to all the body's pivotal points. You can get rid of emotional blocks by releasing whatever emotion you may be suppressing in that layer. Also, you need to take a holistic approach by working with your other energy bodies to conduct a deep emotional cleansing.

Mental Blockage

The mental blockage usually occurs within the mental body, which is another of the seven auric layers. Any blockage in the mental layer, in turn, affects your subconscious mind. Your subconscious handles 90 percent of your thoughts every day, even though you are usually unaware you are having these thoughts. This makes it easy for a mental blockage to happen without you even realizing it. To identify if you have a mental block, the best thing you can do is monitor your thoughts and see how they influence your feelings, actions, and reactions. A blockage in the mental layer can cause a blockage in the emotional layer. So, you need to know what happens in your mind. If there is a pattern of negative thinking, that could be the problem. The solution is to dissolve that pattern and then form a positive one. You must also release the blockage from your mental layer and then repair and help it heal.

Meridian Blockage

Meridians are like little streams that carry energy around the energy bodies in the physical layer. Each meridian has specific qualities attributed to it. When a meridian blockage occurs, it typically affects the qualities. Most times, emotions cause blocks in the meridians; in other words, emotional energy gets blocked in the meridian. So, when working on clearing your emotional body, also take advantage of that moment to clear the meridians. This will make the clearing as in-depth and profound as possible. You can work on attuning the meridians to maintain their health by healing and repairing any fault.

Spiritual Blockage

Spiritual blockage happens in multiple places, so you need to find precisely where the problem is to release it. The spiritual body is vulnerable to energies. It has the tendency of picking up energies outside of its own operations. These are external energies, which usually include imprints, attachments, and implants. Also, when an auric tear occurs, it affects the spiritual body terribly. Blockages in the chakra and other parts of the energy system may also affect the spiritual body. This means that releasing a spiritual blockage need not do with the spiritual body itself. You must find the blockage's source, which could be the chakra, an auric layer, the meridian, etc.

Relationship Blockage

Psychic blocks sometimes occur due to your interpersonal relationships. This blockage is one of the most difficult to access and release because they usually cross different locations within your energy system. As a result, you may experience an energy imbalance which exacerbates your relationship problems. Relationship blocks are typically found in the emotional and mental energy bodies.

Past Life Blockage

Past life blockage occurs in another reality, yet it affects your present reality. This blockage comes from actions in your past life. They are a spiritual blockage which typically includes soul contracts, family connections, memories, or in the worst cases, curses. To attain spiritual growth in your psychic development journey, you have to work on clearing past life blockages, but if you are too fixated on your past life, it could be a sign of a mental blockage instead. Regardless of what it is, the best thing you can work on is your present reality.

Now that you know how to locate psychic and energy blocks in your system, how do you release the blocks? It is a relatively straightforward process that entails steps. But first, here are signs to tell when developing a blockage.

- Negative thinking pattern
- Self-destructive tendencies
- Stress and anxiety
- A lack of energy
- Lethargic feeling
- Feeling stuck or restricted
- Erratic or unstable feelings and behaviors
- Loss of decisiveness
- Loss of motivation and direction

These are ways that blockages manifest in the body due to negative emotions and disruption of energy flow.

How to Release an Emotional Blockage

Meditation is one of the most effective ways to release any emotional block. But the process goes beyond a simple meditative process. You may need to perform the steps we will be discussing a couple of times before you finally get rid of the block.

There are five steps in the meditative exercise. Before you begin, find a quiet place where you won't be interrupted or bothered while doing the exercise. Then, assume a sitting position that is both stable and comfortable. The best thing is to sit upright on a chair or on the floor, whichever you prefer, but a chair is more likely to be comfortable in the long run. Floors become cold quickly. Be relaxed and gently close your eyes. For at least one minute, simply sit in that position and focus on your breathing. You may use a mantra or choose not to. Sit in this relaxed position for some time and then begin releasing your emotional block (s).

Locate the Emotion

The first step is to locate the emotion. With your eyes closed, ruminate on experiences that might have triggered an adverse reaction or feeling in you. It could be that time when you argued at work, or maybe a time when someone mistreated you, and you felt resentment. For at least 30 seconds, think about the incident that comes to mind first. Try to remember in detail as vividly as possible. At that moment in time, you are an observer rather than a participant. You are witnessing what happened from a different perspective. By doing this, you can see the emotion you expressed during that incident. Identify the exact feeling you experienced at that moment. Put a label on the feeling. The label should be precise and specific.

Become Aware of the Experience

Slowly, move your attention away from the label you come up with. Move your attention to your physical body and become aware of the sensations it is producing. The sensations are arising from the emotion you have just identified, so pay attention to them. These two things you are experiencing at this moment - a label in your mind and the physical sensations in your body - are the accurate representation of what an emotion is. You cannot separate one from the other because emotions are both a cognitive and physiological experience. That's why emotions are called feelings because you can feel them in your body as you experience them. Pay attention to your body as you remember the experience. Notice every part of your body where the sensations are building up. It may be pressure on your chest or tightness in your guts. You may even feel pressure in your throat. Every point where you feel these sensations is where the emotion is suppressed, causing a psychic block.

Express the Emotion

Once you find the suppressed emotion, you must express it. To do this, place your hand on the part of your body where you have the most intense or noticeable sensation. This is the exact place where the block is. If you notice there is more than one location for the block, move your hand from location to location until you reach all the points. As you reach each location, take a moment and say, "It hurts here," out loud. Expressing physical discomfort means that a part of you is out of balance, physically, mentally, and spiritually. Your body also knows this balance, but it cannot resolve the imbalance itself.

Accept Responsibility

We suppress emotions because we don't want to accept responsibility for experiencing that emotion. Often, this is due to a negative connotation associated with the emotion. For example, anger is stereotypically regarded as a negative emotion. Anger can be positive and negative; it all depends on how you respond to it. So, take responsibility for the feelings blocked within your body. Accept that the experience is happening in your own body. This means you are the one in control of the emotion, not the other way around. Accepting responsibility means that you recognize that you are the one in control of how you respond to emotional triggers. Unless you accept responsibility, you cannot release the emotional block from your body.

Release the Emotion

After accepting the responsibility for the emotion responsible for your psychic block, the next step is to release that emotion. Once again, pay attention to the parts of your body where the emotion is suppressed. Then, with every breath that goes in and out of your body, make an intention of releasing the emotion. Every time you take a breath, repeat your intention to let go. As you do this, you will feel the tension and pain evaporating from your body. If you need to, you can make audible sounds that resonate in the location of the emotion. This can help loosen and get rid of the contraction.

Just like that, you got rid of the emotional block preventing you from accessing your psychic abilities. You can use this exercise whenever you have an experience that triggers a negative emotion for you. Doing this will prevent other emotional blocks from forming and obstructing your spirituality.

Other Ways of Releasing Psychic Blocks

Besides this exercise for releasing emotional blockages, there are other ways you can release all types of psychic blockages.

- **Clear External Energy Sources:** Your energy source is usually open, so other people can tap from your power source. When this happens, your aura shrinks and becomes susceptible to external energies around you. Think of this as you think of germs invasion on the immune systems. The same thing happens to your energy. Sometimes, foreign energies come into your field and get stuck. This can be very uncomfortable for you because foreign energy bodies' composition differs from your own. It can cause tears, leaks, and distorted energy in your auric layers. It can even block and shut down your chakra system. Even worse, it can shut down your connection to Spirit. So, clearing foreign energy from your energy field is one of the most effective ways to release blocks.

• **Remove Hooks**: Hooks form in your energy field when you play power games with another person, and they invade your energy field, resulting in tears, leaks, and blockages. It feels like having someone's body part anchored to your energy field for no reason. Cutting the hook is crucial to accessing Spirit.

• **Cut Cords:** There are negative cords of attachment that form when you continuously spend time with negative people. These cords sink your vibrations to the lowest frequency. When a cord attaches your energy field to a negative person's energy field, your best bet is to cut the cord and free your energy. It is not even ideal to have an open channel between two fields. It does not matter whether one field is harmful or not.

• **Clear Chakras:** If your chakra system is blocked, you need to open and clear them. Even if it only affects one chakra, you need to open each of the chakras. Unless all the chakras are opened, you cannot align and balance them. It is essential to clear up your chakras regularly, regardless of blocks, because they connect to vital glands, organs, and areas in your life. Clean chakras facilitate positive experiences.

- **Use Crystals:** Crystals have cleaning and healing power. That means they can help you eliminate blocks and repair tears and leaks in your energy field. They can help you release stuck energy to improve the overall energy flow in your field. Place the crystals on your chakras and use a visualization exercise to clear the blockage and restore energy flow.

- **Reiki Healing:** Energy healing is a way of clearing out stuck, leaky, or blocked energy from the energy bodies or the energy field. You may need to visit a Reiki energy healer to use this method. It is a simple process, so you can even learn it for yourself. All it involves is placing your hand inches away from your aura while using it to move energy in the appropriate parts of your field.

- **Consult Spirit Guides**: Finally, you can contact your spirit guide to help with the psychic blocks. This is possible if you have interacted with the guide before. But even if you haven't, spending Spirit time every day can help you reach out. Use meditation to activate your spiritual connection and contact your spirit guide.

After you release all the psychic blocks that prevent you from accessing your abilities, you can continue using the exercises and techniques above to maintain the health of your aura, chakra, meridian, and other parts of the system blocks likely to occur. You need these to maintain your connection with Spirit, so don't entertain the thought of stopping midway. Work on creating a schedule that allows for daily Spirit time, non-negotiable. Doing this will turn the sessions into a habit, reducing the possibility of stopping mid-way.

In addition, consider using positive affirmations in your daily activities. They help keep negativity far away from you. Also, eat more organic food free from toxins. Healthy, organic foods can help maintain or restore your vitality and energy. Like you, food also has energy fields. So, if you consume foods with toxic energy, it will affect your energy field. Finally, spend daily time in nature. This is an incredible way of harmonizing your energy field. Nature has healing vibrations you can take advantage of to fine-tune your energy pathways and channels.

Chapter Five: Activating the Third Eye and True Mindfulness

You are walking on a path, and your instincts tell you to stop. You get a hunch about an exam question. You know who is calling when your phone rings. You meet a new person and, deep in your gut, you just know they can't be trusted. All these experiences have something to do with your third eye. It is the seat of intuition, so every intuitive experience you have is connected. As you advance in your spiritual journey, you will undoubtedly come to realize this. The more open the third eye is, the stronger and more accurate your intuition is. When it gets to a point, you can even start predicting things before they happen.

Activating it is the key to achieving true mindfulness because when it is open, you always become aware of yourself and everything around you. Activating your third eye isn't something that you do in one go. It is a process, and it may take years before you can finally activate it fully. You are the sole determinant of how long it takes to open fully.

The third eye is located in the center of your forehead, slightly higher than your eyebrows. It is the center of imagination, intuition, and inner wisdom. You can't physically see this since it is a spiritual eye. It is made of energy and connected to the third eye chakra. That center of your head is connected to the pineal gland, responsible for most of its abilities. Opening it requires you to activate the pineal gland. It is rare for people to discuss consciousness without mentioning consciousness. The pineal gland is the seat of human consciousness. Without the pineal gland, you cannot attain your full psychic potentials. The first thing I want to explain in-depth is the connection between the pineal gland and the third eye and how this connection impacts your clairvoyance ability.

The pineal gland is in the middle of your brain, directly behind your eyes. It is pea-sized and comes in the shape of a pinecone. It has a reddish-grey color. The pineal gland used to be a highly critical tool for seers and mystics. But these days, it has become dormant, and its purpose has been lost over the years. Note that consciousness is the link between your body and spirit. This means that the pineal gland, as the seat of consciousness, is the actual link.

The chakra system is the channel through which energy movies within the physical body. It is responsible for the ability of the spirit to animate form. Think of the chakras like the wheels on an engine – by distributing energy around the body effectively, they allow energy to remain balanced and open. This allows for optimal function. If energy becomes stagnant in the chakra system, it affects every part of your body. Potentially, it can cause unease, illness, and depression. Your chakras are your body's energy center, whereas your organs are in defined locations throughout the body. The organs control the chakras, but they are not restricted to one location, unlike organs. For example, whereas your heart organ is on your body's left side, the heart chakra is in the center of your chest. Similarly, the third eye chakra is in the center of your forehead.

In the Hindu chakra system, the pineal gland is called the Ajna Chakra. This is the Hindu name for the third eye chakra. In every esoteric tradition, it is regarded as humans' connection to Spirit. It is the space between you and the Divine, moving you through every human experience stage. An open and healthy third eye is your highest source of ethereal energy. The importance of this goes beyond the "physical" properties. It is transcendent in the way it affects our spiritual journey. Opening your third eye is the key to all psychic abilities, including clairvoyance, telepathy, astral projection, mediumship, and lucid dreaming.

Opening it can benefit you in many ways. One of these ways is that it helps you harness your inner wisdom. An opened third eye opens the path to greater self-awareness and emotional mastery. These are the two bases of inner wisdom. When you open it, you will realize just how much wisdom and intelligence have always been at your fingertips. The more benefits you see, the more inclined you will be towards opening your third eye to the ultimate capacity.

Your third eye can restore your health to optimal function. If you want better health, activating it might be your key to achieving that. An average individual desires a life where they can live without fear, worry, or other similar experiences. Suppose you also wish this life for yourself. In that case, it is nothing you can't achieve by opening your intuition to the fullest capacity.

To activate your third eye, you must make meditation a habit. The power of meditation is that it can change the nature of your thoughts from the very root. This means that you can use meditation to reprogram your cognitive processes, hence manifesting the pattern of thoughts that you want. And when you get rid of the baggage of negative thinking through this, you can attain the highest order of life you desire. Remember the law of attraction - positive attracts positive. By retraining your mind to allow mostly positive thinking and feelings, you can increase your vibration and soar in spirituality. As you open it, your physical, mental, and emotional health will flourish. This helps you attract souls on similar vibrational levels with you - leading to better relationships in all aspects.

Like most people, you probably wonder what is there for you in life. "What awaits me out there?" Even if you don't know what it is, you have no cause for worry. Anything you want to know about your career, dreams, goals, or relationships becomes accessible when you activate your third eye. There is a wealth of information waiting for you in that part of your system. You only need to open and gain access to them. By opening your third eye, you can see the world from a new perspective that is more favorable to you. You can see the unseen and turn the impossible into the possible.

When you first attempt to tune in with it, you might find you can't do it. If this happens to you, it simply means it is blocked. A blocked third eye obstructs your access to intuition, imagination, and infinite wisdom. With a blocked third eye, you have no sense of direction in life. Your energy becomes stuck and stagnant, and so do you. A blocked third eye is the pathway to perpetual unhappiness and apathy. When you have a blocked Ajna, you stop believing in the voice of your inner wisdom. You stop listening to your gut feelings. You lose your connection with your spirit. Your perception of the world may become skewed and distorted.

Since the third eye controls your body's neurological functions, you will notice your body loses some ability when it becomes blocked. The body may become unable to regulate sleep, metabolic balance function, or fight infection. Consequentially, you will find yourself getting sick frequently. You may have insomnia, or in worse cases, develop high blood pressure. Some signs of a blocked third eye include:

- Narrow-mindedness
- Lack of direction in life
- Loss of imagination
- Denial
- Poor vision

- Poor memory

Sometimes, the third eye may not be blocked but is overactive. When it is overactive, you will get signs that include:

- Obsession with psychic vision
- Hallucinations
- Paranoia
- Inability to focus
- Nightmares
- Random blankness
- Increased skepticism

You may also experience lucid dreams due to an overactive or imbalanced third eye.

When you notice it is blocked, you must work on unblocking it. This is sometimes a long process. But if you know the right things to do, you can eventually open it fully. There are three ways you can open the third eye: foods, affirmations, and meditation techniques.

Third Eye Foods

The food you consume has a significant impact on the health of your third eye. With the right diet, you can even enhance your intuitive and perceptive abilities. This is not a thrill. Your third eye thrives on brain food, especially those with a purple or indigo-like appearance. The pigment of this color represents every dream, idea, value, and connection to the universe. Below are some of the best foods you can consume to aid the activation of your third eye. These foods are nutritional, plus they can help balance your third eye and jumpstart your journey into the realm of higher consciousness.

- Blueberries, blackberries, and similar fruits with purple pigments contain antioxidants. Their color also reflects that they contain flavonoids, particularly resveratrol, which decreases blood pressure. Circulation instantly becomes better when the arterial walls are relaxed. Antioxidants help relax them, and that improves the circulation to your pineal gland.

- Plums and prunes are also great for the awakening of the third eye. They contain another type of antioxidant called phenols. These can neutralize any harmful radical that wants to worm its way into the brain cells and molecules. Remember that the pineal gland is in the center of the brain, so whatever affects the brain cells will affect it.

- Vegetables such as purple kale, purple cabbage, purple onions, and eggplants are more examples of food that should be in your diet for third eye-opening and activation. These vegetables contain polyphenols, which reduce inflammation.

- Although they don't have purple pigments, fish, nuts, and flaxseed are also great for your third eye. They supply your body with Omega-3s, thereby reducing your risk of schizophrenia, depression, dementia, and dyslexia.

- Dark chocolate is scientifically proven to help with mental clarity. It triggers the release of serotonin, the feel-good hormone, which inadvertently improves your ability to focus. It is no wonder why so many people enjoy chocolate.

Your third eye's energy center regulates the functions of your brain, eyes, ears, nose, and neurological system. You need to allow blood flow to these critical areas as they help keep your chakra system in balance. Suppose you often experience migraine, dizziness, depression, eye strain, insomnia, and hallucination. There, it is a sign you need to switch to a healthier diet that helps your third eye. So, when next you visit the grocery store, look out for purple fruits and vegetables and make sure they are fresh. You have no excuse for not feeding your intuition with the right diet.

Third Eye Affirmations

Apart from food, affirmations can help open your third eye. Positive affirmations have been proven to be almost as effective as meditation in keeping it opened and balanced. They are easy to integrate into your daily routine to clear and balance that area every day. If you remember to do your meditation and affirmations every day, you won't have to worry about it becoming blocked. You can write affirmations down in your journal and recite them every day. Or you can recite them whenever you are having a meditation session. The important thing is to be consistent with the practice. That is the surest way to get results. Below are powerful affirmations you can use to open it and tune in with your intuition and inner wisdom.

- I am intuitive, wise, and aligned with my inner wisdom
- I am connected to my inner wisdom and higher consciousness
- I trust in the power of my intuition
- I seek to learn from the deep wisdom of my higher consciousness
- I am in tune with the infinite wisdom of the Divine
- I see and act in line with my divine purpose
- I open myself to my deepest wisdom and inner guidance
- I am unstoppable in my capacity for joy, happiness, and healing
- I release and let go of the past
- I embrace new energy, new places, new people, and new experiences

- I am illuminated by the light of my higher mind
- I am the source of love, joy, and truth in my life

You can take it a step further and form your affirmations by yourself. The key is to make sure they are positive and directed at yourself. Follow the examples above when forming your affirmations. The best thing about affirmations is that you can craft them to specific areas of your life you want to change. For example, you could say, "The light of the Divine illuminates my career." Or you can make it even more specific and say, "My presentation today is illuminated by the light of the Divine. As I tap into my inner wisdom, all is well with my presentation."

Recite the affirmations twice every day. Meditation should also be practiced twice every day, once in the morning and once in the evening.

Meditation Techniques for the Third Eye

Meditation is one of the first things that should come to mind whenever you want to do anything that involves strengthening your psychic abilities. It is one of the fastest and most effective ways to get your third eye to open. There are plenty of meditation techniques for opening it, but I will only give you three powerful ones. These techniques are simple and straightforward, so don't worry about being a beginner. You will find them easily, even if you haven't tried meditation or mindfulness before.

Here is a simple technique you can start with:

- Find a nice and quiet place for meditation. Make sure it is somewhere you are unlikely to be interrupted by anyone. Switch off your mobile gadgets and any other distracting objects near you.

- Sit in a comfortable position. You may sit on a chair with your back in an upright position and your feet firmly on the floor.

- Gently breathe in and breathe out at least ten times. Make sure the breaths are deep and slow.

- Direct your attention to the space between your eyebrows, which is where you have your third eye. Focus on this space as you continue to inhale and exhale.

- Now, visualize a purple orb of energy in this location. Remember that purple is the third eye's color, so don't exercise with any other color.

- As you inhale and exhale, imagine the purple orb of energy expanding and getting bigger and warmer.

- Picture it is purging all forms of negative energy from your third eye.

- Visualize yourself, absorbing the warmth from the orb - feel as it washes all over you.

- When you are confident that you have fully absorbed the energy, open your eyes.

The above is a simple meditation exercise easy to incorporate into your daily routine. It should not take over 10 to 15 minutes each day. But suppose you wish to make it longer. There, you can visualize the energy orb going from one part of your body to another and purging them of negativity.

Here is another meditation technique for opening the third eye. This is a more prolonged technique, so it may take you 30 to 60 minutes. It is a yoga technique, so be sure to follow the instructions carefully and precisely.

Instructions

- Find a quiet and relaxing place to meditate.

- Inhale deeply via your nose. Wait a few moments, then exhale via your mouth.

- Relax your face as you inhale and exhale. Feel as the relaxation extends to the rest of your body.

- Slowly, relax more and more.

- Concentrate on the middle of your forehead. Feel the energy of the third eye as you focus on that point. Feel as it radiates purple light.

- Visualize the light traveling out of your third eye in 360 degrees.

- Release all harmful and disruptive thoughts to the radiating light.

- Continue to relax your face and body.

- Imagine the sphere of light in your forehead opening. Watch as it radiates.

- Notice the physical sensations in your body as it becomes lighter.

- Let the third eye open as you relax your body, and it becomes lighter.

- Ask the Divine to bestow pure white light on you. Ask that the light fills every part of you and every place around you.

- Take your time before you open your eyes.

Make sure you follow the instructions for this technique carefully.

The Trataka Technique

The Trataka meditation technique is also called the third eye meditation because it specifically opens and activates the third eye. It involves focusing all your awareness on your third eye to enter a meditative state instantly. This is not one of those meditations you can do anywhere, like on the bus or in transit. The best way to do it is when you are as still as possible.

- Assume the lotus position (cross-legged). If you cannot maintain this pose without getting uncomfortable, sit on the chair as you would typically do when meditating.

- Sit upright so your spine is as straight as possible. Then, close your eyes gently.

- Slowly breathe in and out three times.

- Focus on the center of your forehead.

- With your eyes closed, look upwards about 25 degrees above. This is the spot of the third eye.

- Slowly, count from a hundred to one (backward, 100, 99, 98...).

- Do not take your eyes away from the center as you count backward.

- Soon, you will feel a sweet strain in your eyes. It may be a strain, but it will be a pleasant one; you will enjoy it.

- As you near the end of your counting, you will notice a strange sensation around the place where your third eye is. You may struggle to describe the sensation with a specific word. Focus on the third eye location.

- Eventually, you will achieve a state of stillness where it feels like you can see your thoughts. They may appear to you like they are moving on a screen.

- After some moments, your thoughts will stop moving, and you can see them. You may feel like you are in a trance or having a dream.

- Remain in this state for at least 10 minutes.

- Then, slowly return yourself to a state of normalcy. Let the strain on your eyes go, and slowly shift your eyes back to their normal position. They will feel loose and free. Direct your consciousness away from the third eye location.

- Remain still for some minutes. Allow your eyes to feel like themselves once again. Then, breathe in and out three times again.

- Slowly, open your eyes and return to your regular business.

- Your meditation is complete.

This meditation is an effective technique for strengthening your third eye. Besides this, the exercise helps your physical eyes. It protects them from potential damage. Note that the strain you feel during the exercise cannot affect your eyes. Practice this meditation every morning and evening. It will help you develop your intuition with each practice.

Precaution: Be aware that this meditation technique is a very sensitive exercise. Remember that it focuses on one aspect of your subtle bodies. When you meditate, you may notice that the middle of your forehead starts heating up. If this happens, stop the meditation immediately and try again on another day.

If you are consistent with your practice, you will start seeing signs that your third eye is opening and activating. However, if you aren't already aware of these signs, you may mistake them for something else. To avoid that, here are common third eye awakening signs to watch out for.

• **Dull Sensation**: You will start getting a dull sensation in the middle of your forehead. This generally begins when the third eye opens. The sensation results from your consciousness opening. It may feel like someone is lightly tapping you in that center, or there will be a spread of warmth around that area. This sensation might not appear while you are doing your third eye meditation. It often appears out of nowhere, so just keep an eye out for it.

• **Increased Intuition**: This is one of the most apparent signs of third eye awakening. You don't even have to look out for it because you are bound to notice the changes. When the third eye opens, you will experience an increase in intuitive abilities. Usually, intuition happens randomly. You may not even realize it when it comes. But when your third eye is awakening, you will notice that your intuition has become stronger and more dominant. It is no longer random. It is now like a compass guiding you every step of the way. For example, you might know the next step of action with no explanation. Don't fight your intuition when this starts happening. Instead, tune in with it and accept it for what it is.

• **Sensitivity to Light and Color**: With the awakening of your third eye, you might find you have become more sensitive to light and bright colors. The process is usually subtle and mild, but you should be able to notice when it starts. This newfound sensitivity to light and color is a way of further becoming hyper-aware of everything around you. It is a sign you are on the road to achieving true mindfulness.

• **Gradual Change**: The point of opening your third eye is to help you gain a new and profound perspective on the universe, and that is precisely what will happen to you. You will notice slow and steady changes in your outlook on life and your personality. These changes will be beneficial to your life so just embrace them as they come. The way you treat people, animals, nature, and everything else around you will change. You might become less selfish and more tolerant of others. This is one benefit of awakening your third eye.

• **Frequent Headaches**: With an open third eye comes increased headaches. This pressure on your head will be even stronger than the pressure we described in the first bullet point. The headache usually happens because of energy overload from the opening of the third eye. You can use the energy to meditate, take a walk with nature, or do anything else that you enjoy. Headaches are actual signs that your spiritual eye is opening, and the pineal gland is activating.

As your third eye continues to open and awaken, you may experience things that will seem strange to you at first. If you aren't careful with your approach, you are likely to become overwhelmed. This may cause you to struggle with your new abilities. You can manage these experiences with careful planning to not cause an overload of intuitive hits for you.

• **Sleep Disruption**: Opening the third eye means you will start having frequent vivid dreams and nightmares. This can severely mess with your sleep. The intense dreams and nightmares can keep you up all night. This may cause you to wake up feeling fatigued and tired. Even during the day, the images from your dreams or nightmares might keep returning to your mind. To avoid this happening, meditate every night before you go to sleep. Doing this will keep your mind in a calm and relaxed state, reducing your possibility of having an intense dream or nightmare.

And you can keep a dream journal to understand recurring patterns from your dreams or nightmares. Sometimes, these dreams don't stop coming because you must interpret their meaning. Once you interpret the message or lesson, your third eye will stop hitting you with intense imagery.

- **Astral Projection:** This is a spiritual journey where your astral body leaves your body to go elsewhere. Your body can explore any part of the universe, including the higher planes, in an astral state. As your third eye opens and becomes more powerful, you may start astral projecting unpredictably. If you have never astral-projected, the first time might be very frightening for you. But if you understand that astral projection isn't inherently dangerous, you will be fine. Should you fear never finding your physical body again, know this only happens in movies. You can't get stuck outside. Astral projecting is a sign you are attaining psychic development as you desire.

To conclude, below is a highlight of everything you should do daily to help your third eye remain opened and balanced.

- Meditate for at least 10 minutes every morning and evening
- Use essential oils on your pulse points
- Sleep for approximately 8 hours every night
- Eat nourishing, third eye-friendly foods
- Recite positive third eye affirmations every morning and evening

With these, you can keep your third eye open, activated, and balanced.

Chapter Six: How to Intuit and Read the Energy of Those Around You

Energy is the force of life coursing through everything in the universe. As I stated in a previous chapter, everything in the universe is made of energy. The universe itself is energy, along with its many entities and manifestations of energy forms. From this, you can tell it is one of the most vital elements in the world. Learning to read it gives you the ability to unravel a person to their very core. If you know how to read energy, you can see beyond the outer persona most people project. You will access the real person within. As you can see, this is an exciting thing to learn.

Energy reading is the ability to sense and interpret a person's energy field. As established, everyone has a field unique to them. Thoughts and emotions influence this field. Therefore, if you learn to read energy, you learn to read others' thoughts and feelings. Whether you do this with or without their knowledge is your decision to make. But the morally right thing to do is never to use your energy reading power to gain access to people's deepest secrets unless they give you their consent.

The concept of energy reading has existed for centuries. Throughout history, there have been reports of people who use their energy reading skills to uncover man's deepest secrets. Someone who can sense and read other people's energy is a highly intuitive person, a psychic. Therefore, to read energy means to intuit. Highly intuitive people are sensitive to the flow of the life force within the universe. They can pick up the subtlest fluctuation in an individual's energy field, place, animal, or object. Sometimes, energy reading is called aura reading because of the similarities between the two. You can also use them interchangeably.

If you are wondering if energy reading is the same as psychic reading, it is not. But psychics also can do energy readings since the primary tool is intuition. Anybody with a strong sense of intuition can do a reading. The main difference between energy reading and psychic reading is that. In contrast, energy reading focuses on the sensory organs. Psychic reading involves connecting with a nonphysical realm. Also, energy reading observes the aura to get information, whereas psychic reading contacts spirit guides.

Suppose you have been where you meet someone new, and you instantly don't like them. There, you have experienced a classic example of your intuition picking up on the other person's energy. If yours doesn't align with that of another person, you will likely feel detached from them. To some extent, we are all energy readers because we can discern if a person is good or bad based on how they make us feel when we meet them. Understandably, when this happens, we don't realize that the feelings we are picking up are from their energy field. Energy readers are not very different from you. The difference is that they have refined and worked on their abilities. If you polish yours too, you might become as good as your average energy reader.

Learning to intuit can be great for you. Whenever you feel or get stuck in life, you can count on your energy reading ability to tell you what is wrong. For instance, if you keep working on a project without making headway, doing an energy reading will tell you why. Everything that happens in your life is somehow linked to the force flowing within you. So, it is not such a bad idea to turn to energy reading whenever you feel lost or stuck.

If you are having a hard time making an important decision, an energy reading can help you decide. Whether the decision is about your career, love life, or business, it is a handy way of knowing what to do. With it, you can gain a deeper insight into the events of your life. Based on your energy field, you can discover the right path to tow in life.

What do you gain when you learn to read energy?

- Receive divine guidance
- Recognize areas of your life that need immediate and special attention
- Detect and get rid of energy blocks. This further strengthens your intuition
- Energy reading can help you deal with trauma from the past
- Get enough insight and information about yourself
- Gain a new perspective on life and its challenges
- Balance your chakras

There are many more things you can benefit from learning to read your energy. Still, those are some benefits people who have tried it talk about the most.

Emotions are the most common expressions of energy. They are the "vibe" you give off to people and get from people. It goes both ways. You feel good when you are around some people, but other people make you feel uncomfortable. Energy flow is manifested through a person's emotions. When you come across someone with a positive energy flow, you are likely to feel happy and good. But someone with a negative energy flow will make you feel stressed, anxious, exhausted, and uncomfortable.

Emotional energy is a highly crucial thing. It is contagious. The difference between a healthy and toxic relationship is emotional energy. Before you interact with anyone regularly, it won't hurt to get a read on them and learn their life force. You will then know whether a friendship, romantic relationship, or even a business relationship is feasible to establish with such a person. In other words, you check your energy compatibility. It is similar to how we study someone's behavior to see how compatible we are when thinking of dating or marriage.

Unfortunately, some people are good at hiding who they are at the beginning of a relationship. So, studying their behavior may not give you anything tangible. But if you know how to read energy, they can't hide their energy from you. When you read them, you can tell whether their words and actions match their energy. If it doesn't, then you know that they are hiding something. With reading energy, what you see is what you get.

Here are some examples of a person's energy not correlating with their words or behavior.

- You have a fight with your partner. You both apologized to each other, but somehow, you can still sense hostility from them.

- A person is asking you out in the most romantic way possible, but you simply don't feel the genuineness. You can tell there is not much heart there.

- A friend is being cheerful and acting like sunshine, but you don't sense happiness from them. Instead, you get the feeling that they are hurting deep inside.

Ultimately, the energy you feel from someone tells you the truth about who they are and where they are. This means that you should know how to link it with their emotions. Some people are not trying to be deceptive or misleading. Whatever the project is unintentional because they may not even be aware of what they feel. If they tell you something, it will be because they believe it, not because they deliberately want to mislead you. The good thing is this doesn't matter since you can still decode their true emotions.

Here, the key is to pay attention and concur to the messages you receive from your body. Naturally, your mind may want to convince you of something else. Don't allow yourself to be talked out of the wisdom of your body. To understand this better, here is something you can do. When figuring your energetic response to people out, always pay attention to how your body feels. Does your energy soar, or does it take a sudden dip? Rather than resisting the message from your body, follow its lead. So, how do you read people's emotions through their energy?

Sense Their Presence

This means the energy they emit - the energy that does not necessarily match their words or actions. An emotional atmosphere surrounds each person. Tune in to this atmosphere to get insight into a person. In this context, presence may also be interpreted as their charisma - the magnetic force you are drawn to in people. Know the fact that charisma does not always contain heart for some people. Be wary of people like this as they often turn out to be bad for you.

An example would be a narcissist. Narcissists can be energy vampires because they seek highly intuitive and sensitive people like you and milk them of their force. Narcissists are often so charismatic, making it hard to determine their true intentions. You can trust nobody who has charisma without heart. They are likely to be deceptive in most cases, if not all cases.

As you try to sense a person's presence, pay attention to these things:

- How warm or cold is their energy?
- Do you feel like your energy is draining around them?
- Is there a friendly warmth that pulls you to them?
- Can you sense distractibility?

Watch Their Eyes

The eye is a very powerful organ. So much information can be exchanged through the eyes. If someone hates your gut, you can tell from their eyes. On the contrary, if they want to shower you with love, it is also in their eyes. The eyes convey powerful energies - the Poet Rumi calls this, "The glance." Just like the brain, the eyes also project powerful electromagnetic signals. These signals are the reason you can sometimes feel like you are being watched even when there is nobody around.

Hunters, soldiers, and police officers report this every time. The power of the energies transmitted through the eyes is also why some cultures have what you know as the "evil eye." This is believed to be a powerful gaze that can inflict bad luck on the recipient.

Pay attention to the eyes of people you encounter. Are they mean? Nice? Angry? Tranquil? Sexy even? Note that the face differs from the eyes. A person can have a mean look while their eyes look gentle. The way people look at you can make you experience a range of responses. Someone can make you feel happy, adored, frightened, or angry with their eyes. Also, try to see whether they are guarding their emotions.

But when you look into people's eyes, don't look too deeply. Some people's eyes have a hypnotic effect. If you don't trust an individual, don't look deep into their eyes. The less engagement you have with negative energy people, the less likely they will zone in on your energy levels. On the other hand, with someone you trust and feel comfortable with, look into all their eyes. Let their beautiful energy wash all over you.

Observe How a Touch, Hug, and Handshake Make You Feel

Energy is usually transmitted through physical contact. It is similar to how electric currents flow through cords and cables. Physical contact with someone can tell you a lot about their feelings or intention towards you. Notice how it feels when you hug someone. Does it feel warm? Confident? Off-putting? Comfortable? Are the hands sweaty or clammy? Is the grip super strong to where you feel crushed? Whatever you feel from the physical contact can give you an insight into their emotions and state of mind.

Along with the physical clues, the vibe you receive can also reveal the emotions. When some people shake you, they impart feelings of joy, kindness, or calm. In contrast, some people transmit hostility, clinginess, or even drain you quickly. Be wary of people who drain you of your force. Spending too much time with them can deplete your energy supply. If a person's energy doesn't feel good to you, avoid physical contact of all forms with them.

Notice Their Tone

When someone laughs or talks, listen to their tone. The tone and volume of the person's voice can reveal a lot about their emotions. Vibrations are created by sound frequencies. You hear frequencies loudly. If you don't hear them, you can feel them below an audible range. Observe how the tone of voice or laughter from different people affect you. Words are carried by the energy of people's tone, the warmth, and the coldness.

Listen to see if a person's tone feels soothing, whiny, snippy, or abrasive. Is their tone loud? Do they mumble or talk softly? Is there a slow monotone in the way they talk? The way people laugh suggests lightheartedness. Ask yourself: Does this person's laughter sound genuine? Fake? Catty? Child-like? Heavy? Notice the pitch of their tone and how it makes you feel.

Focus on Their Overall Vibe

Besides the voice, eyes, and touch, try to get a sense of their overall vibe. What do you feel when you are in the same place as this person? What is the energy they emit telling you? Where is it coming from? Is it from a place of concern or care? Is the vibe you are getting positive? Do they radiate kindness to you? Or are you getting the feeling they may be deceptive or mischievous? Energy doesn't lie, so whatever you sense from their overall vibe is likely the real insight on them.

Reading energy is easy, but you must do it the right way. The following are tips for reading someone you have just met.

- **Connect:** The first thing you should do when you meet someone is to extend your goodwill to them. You do this by greeting the person warmly and positively. Doing this allows you to establish a connection with them. More importantly, it helps ensure that you form no conscious or unconscious opinions about them. You need to make sure you have formed no judgment about the person you are reading. The importance of this cannot be overemphasized, so take it very seriously. Forming judgments beforehand, whether positive or negative, can be a hindrance to a clear reading. You must be as neutral as possible.

- **Set Intent:** What do you want to know about the person you are reading right now? This is something you should ask yourself to focus on your intention. This question is simple yet deliberate. It implies that you want information about the person at that moment. This question is crucial because it allows you to filter the information you get from your reading. Think of it as asking for intuitive guidance. That is exactly what it is.

Humans are complex, so there is so much, maybe too much, information to know about the people you meet. Most of the information has nothing to do with your relationship with them, so you don't need that much information. This means you must set your intention to consciously accept just the information relevant to your present relationship with them. It makes any signal you receive stand out to you.

Listen: Center yourself. Pay attention to anything that comes up during your reading. Every thought, feeling, and image you get relevant to what you seek to know, acknowledge them without judgment. Don't think about the importance or nonimportance of what you receive, just receive it. For many people, the main barrier to using their intuition is the inability to develop trust. You are always receiving intuitive information regardless of your personal feelings. You just need to be open to hearing it.

Yet, many people dismiss their intuition without even attempting to listen to it. They think that intuitive information is imaginary, irrelevant, or illogical. Don't be like this. Before you dismiss any information you receive from a person, be curious about how it could help you. Trust that the information came to you for a specific reason, even though you don't know that reason yet.

- **Observe:** Pay attention to how you feel about the information you receive. Even though we like to believe that we have a solid individual identity, all humans have a porous interpersonal boundary. Tapping into these boundaries makes you susceptible to other people's energy, feelings, and thoughts. If you develop your self-awareness to a certain level, you can know exactly what is going on with someone by observing how you feel when you are around them. This goes back to everything we discussed emotion, tone, physical contact, eyes, and overall vibe.

To become a skilled energy reader, you need to train yourself to discern what you pick from people from your energy. Using your intuition to read people is simple and straightforward. The more you practice, the better you will become at intuitively reading.

You don't need psychic readings to know what you want about the people around you. Your intuition is enough. Your ability to intuitively read people goes back to your third eye. Without activating it, your intuition remains at the basic level. Therefore, work on activating your third eye to read energy successfully.

Chapter Seven: Getting to Know the Chakras

Earlier, I mentioned that chakras are the body's invisible energy centers. Still, I didn't go in-depth into what makes them the energy centers. In this chapter, we will be talking in-depth about chakras and their importance to psychic abilities.

In your body system, you have many chakras. However, the most known are the seven that make up the chakra system. If you are not new to spirituality, you have probably heard people say they want to "unblock" their chakras, implying that they can be blocked or opened. Or maybe you have seen Facebook posts where people talked about using stones and crystals to balance their chakras. When they are open, energy flows through them freely, harmonizing the physical body, the mind, and the spirit. The literal translation of "Chakra" in Sanskrit is "wheel," which is why I told you to think of them like the wheels on an engine. When you visualize them, you should have an image of wheels flowing with vital energy.

Allow me to take you through a quick rundown of what chakras are.

You have a physical body. Your physical body has a soul within. But that is not all. Besides your physical body, you also have an energy body, which is the aura. The next chapter is about auras, so I'm not going in-depth into auras right now. As you can tell from the name, your aura is an energetic blueprint of your physical body. The point here is that you have an energy body apart from the physical body you are very familiar with.

The seven chakras are points of energy across your whole system, which is why they are also called energy centers. They process energy and allow it to flow freely to every part of your body. The seven chakras don't all process energy for one aspect of functioning. Instead, they all have a specific area to which they are attached. Your chakras are super sensitive to your thoughts and emotions and past traumas linked to feelings and emotions. Most people assume that health is purely physical, and that is why they let their mental health suffer. They neglect their thoughts and emotions because they believe they don't have a major effect, but that is not correct at all.

Suppose you have a stomach issue that has been there since you were a teenager. Everyone knows that you have a sensitive stomach. Aside from this, you don't feel in control of your life. Your parents are always telling you to do things their way. Even though you don't like others dictating your life for you, you believe that you have a responsibility to follow orders from your parents and other authority figures. You suppress the way you feel about your situation. What is the connection between this and your stomach issue? Nothing, right? Wrong! These two are closely related, but you don't realize it yet.

Because of other people exercising control over your life without your consent, you have cultivated negative programming about your power. Your parents are dictating your life, leaving you without personal power, which can be a problem. Then, your solar plexus chakra becomes blocked due to your suppression of the emotions you are feeling from having your power taken away by the authority figures in your life. You don't know it, but this manifests in your physical body as your sensitive stomach problem. So, you can see how your physical body, mind, and spirit are connected. The chakras hold the connection among these three things, so they are essential for your overall wellbeing.

Root Chakra

The first chakra along the energy system is the root chakra, which you can find at the base of your spine. It is the first to develop in your energy system. It is a representation of your basic and primal instinct, which is to survive. Your root chakra is concerned with your security, safety, and stability, hence its proximity to the earth so you can always remain grounded. Suppose you have a stable relationship, career, and overall stable life. There, it indicates that your root chakra is in a good state. Its proximity to the earth allows you to be self-aware and present.

When the root chakra is balanced, you are likely to feel safe, secure, grounded, centered, and happy. In a scenario where it is underactive and unable to function at an optimal level, it means there is a blockage. Some symptoms of a blockage include fear, anxiety, uncertainty, financial instability, and detachment. You also become disconnected from the physical. Sometimes, it may also become overactive. When this happens, it means this chakra is dominating every part of your life. It affects the way you interact with the world and the people within it.

Symptoms of an overactive root chakra include aggressiveness, materialism, greed, cynicism, and a thirst for power. Blockage and imbalance in the root chakra physically manifest as:

- Constipation
- Eating disorders
- Lower back problems
- Sciatica

- Pain in the legs

Red is the color of the root chakra. The adrenal gland is the connecting gland. Typically, any red-colored gemstone can be used for repairing and healing it.

Sacral Chakra

The sacral chakra develops after the root chakra, which makes it second in the chakra system. It is below the navel, at the point where you have your reproductive organs. From this, you can probably guess it controls your sexual desires, creative power, and connection to people. Having it balanced and healthy means you live a highly creative and joyous life. It also means you have a zest for life. You like to explore and make discoveries about the world around you. You are comfortable with your sexuality, and you have a healthy sexual relationship with your partner. Intimacy comes easily to you, and you don't deny yourself life's many pleasures.

A balanced and healthy sacral chakra manifests as passion, openness, creativity, optimism, and a healthy libido. When blocked or underactive, it will show signs that include:

- Low libido
- Lack of creativity
- Inability to form intimate relationships
- Dysfunctional relationships
- Feelings of being isolated
- Sexual identity disorder

Where the sacral chakra is hyperactive, you may get symptoms that include:

- Addiction to sex
- Manipulative tendencies

- Hedonism
- Overly emotional

If unhealthy or blocked, it will show physical symptoms such as:

- Infertility or impotence
- Sexual dysfunction
- Hip pain
- Erratic menstruation
- Urinary problems

Orange is the color of the sacral chakra. The connecting gland is the Gonads. Gemstones that are orange-colored typically help to repair and heal the sacral chakra. Examples include orange sapphire, carnelian, imperial topaz, etc.

Solar Plexus Chakra

Located just above the navel, the solar plexus is the third chakra in the energy system. It is right in the middle of your stomach area. This is the chakra that gives you the gut feeling or sinking feeling in your stomach. It is also related to intuition, but not in the same way as the third eye. The solar plexus governs your power and your control over your own life. If you feel in charge of your life and every decision you take, that means your solar plexus is in great shape. It makes you feel as free as a bird. People who come from cultures that enforce obedience to authority figures with no questions often have issues with their solar plexus chakra.

When your solar plexus is balanced and healthy, you will naturally feel confident and in control of your life. You also have a very strong personal power and an amazing awareness of self. Plus, you have drive and motivation. But when blocked or underactive, you may get symptoms that include:

- Lack of direction in life
- Low self-esteem
- Inferiority complex
- Heightened sensitivity to criticism
- Feeling of powerlessness

If overactive, it often shows symptoms that include:

- Domineering attitude
- Egoism
- Lust for power
- Perfectionism
- Judgmental

Blockage, cruds, and general problems in the solar plexus physically manifest as:

- Hypertension
- Hypoglycemia
- Sensitive stomach
- Issues with digestion
- Diabetes
- Chronic fatigue

Yellow is the color of the solar plexus chakra. Its connecting gland is the pancreas gland. Yellow-colored gemstones work effectively for healing and balancing it. Examples are yellow sapphire, amber, and citrine.

Heart Chakra

You can find the heart chakra in the center of the chest. It is located next to the physical heart. Remember how that part of your chest feels warm when you think of a loved one? That is the effect of your heart chakra. It is one of the easiest chakras to understand. It controls your capacity to send and receive love. It oversees your relationships, your sense of solidarity with a fellow human, and compassion. If you always find yourself in toxic relationships or fear falling in love, that is a sign that your heart chakra needs to be worked on.

Balance in your heart chakra shows in the way you relate with people around you. Signs of balance include:

- Peace and balanced
- A feeling of loving and being loved
- Tolerance
- Compassion towards other creatures
- Connection to all life in the universe

A blocked or underactive heart chakra may trigger feelings of bitterness and hate in you. A lack of empathy, intolerance, loss of connection with all life, and trust issues are other signs you get when blocked or underactive. If overactive, the symptoms will include:

- Jealousy
- Codependency
- Neediness or clinginess
- Self-sacrifice
- Over-giving

Heart chakra issues physically manifest as:

- Upper back problems
- Heart disease

- Circulatory issues
- High blood pressure
- Lung problems

Green is the color of the heart chakra. Its connecting gland is the thymus gland. Gemstones that are green colored usually work well or clearing and balancing it. Examples include emerald, jade, rose quartz, etc.

Throat Chakra

The throat chakra, as evident from its name, is located in your throat. It is associated with speech and communication. By that, I'm referring to your ability to express yourself in a concise way. It is all about the levels of your communication skills and your self-expression. If you feel like you're having trouble expressing your thoughts and feelings effectively, that is a sign of a problem waiting to be addressed. An open and healthy throat chakra means you have a voice, and you can speak your truth without the fear of criticism.

When balanced, you can see the symptoms. They include:

- Clear communication
- Ability to express yourself without fear or inhibition
- Creativity
- Confidence in giving a speech
- Diplomacy
- Ability to give sound and valuable advice

On the other hand, a blocked or underactive throat chakra will show these symptoms:

- Inability to speak your truth
- Inability to express yourself effectively
- Prone to being misunderstood

- Secretive nature
- Listening or comprehension problems

Where it is overactive, you may show signs such as these:

- Harsh criticism of others
- Overly opinionated
- Gossipy attitude
- Yelling and talking over others
- Problems in the throat chakra may physically manifest as:
- A weak immune system
- Susceptibility to the flu
- Chronic cough
- Sore throat
- Hearing problems

Blue is the color of the throat chakra. The connecting gland is the thyroid gland. Blue-colored gemstones work best for clearing and healing it.

Third Eye Chakra

Since I already talked about the third eye in a full chapter, this will be very brief. As you already know, the third-eye chakra is in the middle of your forehead. It is the most popular chakra due to its link with intuition and psychic abilities. It is the seat of intuition; it is your mind's eye. When it is open and balanced, the symptoms include:

- An active imagination
- High intuition
- Sharp thoughts and a clear mind
- A sense of direction and vision

- Extrasensory perception

A blocked or underactive third eye will show signs like:

- Lack of focus
- Poor creativity and imagination
- Poor memory
- Poor judgment
- Loss of direction
- Lack of extrasensory perceptions

An overactive third eye shows signs that include:

- Hallucinations
- Delusions
- Nightmares and daydreams
- Obsessive thoughts
- Hyperactive extrasensory perceptions

Problems in the third-eye chakra may physically manifest as:

- Poor vision
- Eyestrain
- Headaches
- Poor sleep
- Memory problems
- Lack of concentration

Purple or indigo is the color of the third-eye chakra. The connecting gland is the pineal gland. Purple-colored gemstones are usually effective for clearing and balancing this chakra.

Crown Chakra

The crown chakra is located at the very top of your head, which is called the crown. It is the representation of your connection to the Higher Consciousness. This is the center of spirituality in your body because it is in proximity to your energy source and higher self. It is the channel through which your soul leaves the body when the time comes. When you meditate, this chakra is the one through which you access the universe. When balanced and healthy, it shows symptoms that include:

- Faith in the cosmos
- Connection to the Divine
- A feeling of universal love
- Ability to understand information better
- High intelligence and self-awareness

A blocked and underactive crown shows symptoms that include:

- Isolation and depression
- Learning challenges
- Brain fog
- Disconnection from the spiritual
- Loss of faith

If overactive, the signs usually include:

- Spiritual obsession or addiction
- Judgmental
- Dogmatism
- Ungrounded feelings

Problems here may physically manifest as:

- Neurological problems

- Nerve pain
- Migraine
- Cognitive problems

White is the color of the crown chakra. The connecting gland is the pituitary gland. Any clear-colored gemstones such as amethyst, diamond, or clear quartz can be very effective for clearing and balancing it.

How Chakra Balancing Impacts Psychic Development

To develop or strengthen your psychic abilities, balancing your chakras is one of the vital steps you must take. Without balance, you cannot receive divine guidance or connect with spiritual guides. Keeping them open and balanced is non-negotiable if you want to develop your clairvoyant or psychic ability. You are probably wondering why they have so much importance in psychic development. There are multiple reasons, but I will walk you through the most important three.

Each of your clair senses is linked to a chakra. Your chakras are part of what makes up the energy system. They are your connection with the spiritual realm and the universe. As you already know, opening the third eye is the key to activating your psychic senses. While this is true, the third-eye chakra is not the only one connected with your psychic senses.

More of your chakras are linked to the major psychic senses. If you remember clearly, the four major psychic senses are clairvoyance, clairaudience, clairsentience, and claircognizance.

- Clairvoyance is linked to the third eye chakra
- Clairaudience is linked to the throat chakra
- Clairsentience is linked to the solar plexus chakra

- Claircognizance is linked to the crown chakra

When these chakras are open, clear, and balanced, it means that the portals to these psychic senses are also open and clear. Unblocking them is tantamount to unblocking your psychic portals. And when you form a routine healing practice, you are also enhancing your psychic senses, not just your chakras.

How does this work? The answer to this lies in the second reason.

A balanced energy system is key to receive psychic messages. Chakras are part of the overall energy system. There is a central energy pillar in the energy system that runs through your full spine's length to connect you with the universe through your crown chakra and the earth through your root chakra. Each chakra is similar to a station along the energy pillar and they regulate how it flows through your whole body. To receive psychic messages, the energy pillar, your chakras, and the entire energy system need to be in a clear and clean state. This is to ensure its free flow without blockages.

Let's go back to that windowpane example. Remember that we said the windowpane becomes covered with thick dust? Now, imagine trying to look outside the window with all the dust over it. Will you be able to see anything? Clearly not. You might not even be able to get a peep. Now, imagine when you take your cleaning supplies and get rid of all the dirt and dust on the window. What happens when it becomes clear and shiny? You can immediately see through it into the outside world or inside, depending on your position.

This is the same thing with your psychic senses and your abilities. When there are too many energy blocks and cruds in your chakras, your pathway to receiving psychic messages become obstructed and inaccessible. Therefore, you must make sure that the system remains clean and shiny at all times to achieve psychic development. Remember that cleaning the energy system just once doesn't count. It may work for a while now, but it will eventually become blocked again without constant maintenance. Keeping your chakras open and balanced with regular maintenance exercises is the key to keep receiving psychic messages.

The third reason chakra balancing is crucial to psychic development concerns your energy vibrations. One side effect of clearing your chakras and energy system is that it keeps your vibration high. The universe and everything in it is connected by vital life forces. Still, varying frequency bands exists within the overall force field. Each person's frequency band is the depiction of their reality. If you are a positive person with positive energy, you vibrate at a higher frequency band. Negative energy makes you vibrate at a lower frequency. You are wondering what this concerns your chakras.

Well, chakras mostly become blocked because of negative thoughts, emotions, and energies. The residue of your negative belief system and the scars of your past trauma form blocks in their system. Not only that, but you also allow yourself to continue to vibrate at a lower frequency when you old on traumatic memories from the past. If you can't see how this restricts your ability to receive psychic messages, let me spell it out. Your higher self, angels, and spirit guides are all high vibrational beings, so they exist on a much higher frequency. Suppose you want to connect or communicate with higher vibrational beings in the divine realm. There, you must ensure that you are also operating at a high vibrational frequency. If your frequency is on the lower band, you can't connect with the higher realms.

When you clear your system of all negative thoughts, emotions, and blockages through the chakras, you give positive energy a chance to flow within you. By doing that, you are reducing the gap between yourself and the divine realm.

Clearing and Balancing the Chakras

Clearing your chakras and balancing them is not a one-way thing. There are different ways you can approach chakra alignment. Here, we will discuss the most powerful and easiest ways of balancing them. These include exercises, meditation techniques, routines, and practices you can easily incorporate into your life. You can choose whichever aligns best with your lifestyle, and some methods can even be combined. For example, you can combine meditation with affirmations. Each of the chakras responds to different healing techniques, so we'll look at the exercises one by one.

Note: Refer to Chapter Four for positive affirmations.

Balancing the Root Chakra

If you want your root chakra to remain open, clean, and balanced always, you must make little lifestyle changes. These small changes will cumulate to give you a greater result. First, you must make sure that you get your complete 8 hours of sleep every night. Sound sleep is one way to make sure that your chakra does not get blocked. Then, you must add physical exercises and activities into your daily routine. Your idea of daily physical exercise might be a little gardening every day. Gardening or any other activity that connects you with the earth is, in fact, ideal to help balance it.

Since the root chakra's color is red, you also must incorporate red-colored foods into your diet. Examples include tomatoes, beets, and pomegranates. Consider keeping red gemstones such as garnet or ruby around your environment. They can help boost the vibrancy of your root chakra. Besides the small lifestyle changes, use the exercise below to remain balanced.

- Assume the butterfly pose. Grab your ankles with both hands.

- Next, raise your hips and start rocking back and forth – this will stimulate your perineum area.

- Observe any subtle changes in your body. An example of a change you may experience includes the warming up your body and your hips opening.

- Repeat this exercise 10 to 100 times.

- Don't forget to make yourself comfortable when you do this exercise.

Balancing the Sacral Chakra

The sacral chakra's element is water. Therefore, relaxing near water is one way you can clear and balance its energy. Some of the physical activities you can introduce to your daily routine for this purpose include swimming in natural settings, walking in the rain, or watching rainstorms. Also, introduce more orange-colored fruits and vegetables such as carrots, oranges, etc., in your diet. Goldstone and amber are some of the gemstones you can put around your environment to maintain its energy flow. And this healing exercise is perfect for the sacral chakra.

- Lie flat on your stomach. Place your arms by your side and let your palms face the ground. Point your toes outward.

- Inhale, then raise your right leg upward without bending your knee.

- Exhale as you lower your leg back to the ground. Be slow and gentle when you do this.

- Repeat the movement with your second leg, i.e., your left leg.

- Then, do this movement again with both of your legs simultaneously.

- Repeat until you feel a spread of warmth around your sacral chakra

Balancing the Solar Plexus Chakra

Some of the lifestyle changes you can make to encourage your solar plexus chakra's balance include solving puzzles, reading art books or taking creative classes. The energy of seeing tasks through can help generate positivity. This is the energy that is required to read books or solve puzzles and can help reactivate the solar plexus chakra even when it becomes dormant. Spend more time bathing yourself in the sunshine. To improve your digestion, start a detoxification program. Incorporate more yellow-colored foods such as chamomile and squash into your diet. When you meditate, make sure you have yellow gemstones such as yellow agate and citrine around you. Use yellow essential oils like rosemary to release any blockage.

Along with these changes, incorporate the exercise below in your daily routine.

- Assume the half-lotus pose, with your right leg on top of the left.

- Put your right palm atop your right foot.

- Breathe in and raise your left hand toward the sky. Focus on the back of your hand.

- Breathe out and gently lower your hand back to the top of your foot.

- Repeat this movement with the other hand.

- Alternate between the left and right hand for up to 10 minutes until you feel warm sensations in your solar plexus.

Balancing the Heart Chakra

Inviting pure and positive energy into your life is the surest way to clear and balance your heart chakra. Activities that can help you do this include walking with nature, spending time with your loved ones, or volunteering for charitable organizations. By doing this, you are embracing the feelings of compassion and empathy. This, in turn, awakens your heart chakra and fills it with positivity. Incorporate yellow-colored foods and drinks into your diet. Examples are ginger tea and golden beets. Keep stones such as amber and topaz around your house.

Also, do the exercise below every day.

- Sit in a lotus position.
- Form a fist with your hands and bring them to the front of your chest.
- Inhale deeply. As you inhale, pull your hands back against your chest and expand it as much as you can. Make sure your back is upright as you do this. Remain like this for at least 10 seconds.
- As you exhale, focus back on the center of your body. Curve your spine a little and tuck down your chin.
- Repeat the exercise 10 times, using 10 seconds for each movement.
- You should feel a cool, refreshing feeling spread across your chest as the chakra opens.

Balancing the Throat Chakra

As you already know, the throat chakra is the center of self-expression. Therefore, singing, oral poetry, and meaningful conversations are great activities for balancing it. Any activity that gives room for expressing your thoughts and feelings meaningfully is great for the throat chakra. Also, meditate with blue-colored gemstones to magnify the power of your throat chakra. Besides that, use this exercise to maintain balance and openness.

- Kneel on the ground with your toes curled beneath you. Let your hip rest on your heels.

- Place your hands on your lower back, the place where you have your kidney.

- Breathe in and out gently but deeply.

- As you inhale, slightly bent your body backward as far as it allows while your chin is tilted upward. This will open your throat chakra.

- As you exhale, allow your chin to rest downwards to your chest, making your body cave forward.

- Do this again 10 times until you feel your throat chakra opening and balancing.

Balancing the Third Eye Chakra

Daily meditation is undoubtedly the best way to keep your third eye balanced. Meditation is regarded as the mind's food, and your third eye chakra is the mind's eye. Whatever type of meditation you choose, consider doing it under the sunshine or moonlight. Apart from that, make sure you get enough sleep to improve your mind's clarity and enhance your memory. Indigo-colored foods can also help with your third eye chakra's balancing, so introduce more of them into your diet. Figs and black currants are some foods you can consider.

Follow the sun meditation exercise below to keep it balanced.

- Spread your legs wide apart, bending them about 15 degrees.

- Touch the thumb and index fingers together to form a triangle. Raise your hands upward until your thumbs stop in the middle of your forehead.

- Breathe in and out naturally.

- Then, visualize the sun's energy streaming into your third eye chakra through the triangle you formed.

- Raise your eyes about 15 degrees towards the sky.

- Remain in this position for up to 5 minutes and feel as the sun's energy refreshes your third eye and pineal gland.

Balancing the Crown Chakra

Keeping a dream journal is one way you can train your crown chakra. You can also get a vision board to analyze your dreams and intentions within a spiritually charged space. Meditation is also great because it establishes a link between your physical self and your spiritual body. Make it a habit to visualize a white light source filling the top of your head with energy. Also, eat more cream-colored foods and drinks. Meditate with amethyst, fluorite, and other clear gemstones.

Practice the exercise below to balance your crown chakra.

- Sit comfortably in a half-lotus position. Let your spine sit upright.

- Slowly raise both of your hands and bring them to both sides of your forehead. There should be some space between them.

- Focus on the sensation in the space between your hands.

- Slowly, bring your hands near each other and spread them apart again. To put it simply, expand and contract.

- As you repeat this movement, visualize flowers blossoming with each movement you make.

- Feel the energy flowing through all your chakras.

- Breathe slowly and bring your hand from your head to your lower abdomen in a sweeping motion.

- Continue the meditation for some minutes while your eyes become closed.

Now that you know your seven chakras, the parts of your body they are connected to, and how to balance them, you can recognize a blocked chakra and unblock it quickly. With the exercises and lifestyle changes above, you can live a more balanced life. Balanced chakras will help you maintain the overall energy level you need to connect within yourself and progress in your psychic development journey.

Chapter Eight: Reading Auras

Remember when we talked about a human electromagnetic field in Chapter Six? Well, that electromagnetic field is your aura. The aura is a hazy or blurry bubble of light that extends inches from the body and surrounds it from head to toe. Everything in existence has it, including rocks, books, and other creatures. If energy flows through it, it has an aura. Since we already talked about energy, you already know how the aura works. Itis the same thing as your energy field, therefore, everything discussed energy applies to it. Now, to other aspects of the aura.

The aura has seven layers through which it interacts and relays information with the physical body via the seven chakras. That's right, the chakras are also part of the auric field. Each chakra is connected to each of its layers. Each auric body correlates with your physical, emotional, mental, and spiritual conditions. The vibrations of your thoughts, feelings, health, awareness, and past experiences are stored in each auric body, depending on which one correlates to them.

Its outermost part is the one that typically extends about 5 to 7 feet from the physical body. The degree of extension in each person depends on the overall wellbeing of that individual. Even though you may not be able to see your aura, you can feel it when interacting with another person's aura. This is what it means when you have a clear feeling that another person is within your "personal space." Before you learn how to read the aura, you must recognize and identify the seven subtle energy bodies. This is crucial to reading. Unlike in the previous chapter, where you learned how to use your intuition to read energy, this focuses more on the auric colors. More on this will come later.

Etheric Layer

The etheric body is the closest auric layer to your physical body. It is the one you see when you try to read a person's aura or access their energy for healing. It extends about 2 to 4 inches from the physical body. It may appear to you in the form of a violet or grey fog or mist. The etheric body is connected to your root chakra and your glands, organs, and meridians. It corresponds to the health and state of your physical body. Therefore, any condition that materializes in the physical body often manifests there first. If you learn how to read auras, you can determine when a condition is developing there. Thus, you can take care of it before it materializes physically.

Emotional Layer

The second level of the auric field is the emotional layer, which extends about four inches away from many people's bodies. It encircles the physical body in an oval shape, appearing like a cocoon around it. This part of the aura is connected to the sacral chakra, which is also the second chakra. It primarily relates to your thoughts, feelings, emotions, and experiences.

The emotional body is ever-changing depending on your mood, thoughts, and feeling, and it easily harbors negative emotions such as anger, fear, loneliness, and resentment. Usually, the emotional layer communicates its energies with the etheric layer, which then processes and sends them down to the physical body. When you experience stomach upset, cramps, and physical tension, it is often due to the emotional layer bombarding the etheric body with emotional pain. Since we experience a range of feelings, it normally appears as a mix of all the rainbow colors. By reading it, you can easily determine the state of your chakras.

Mental Layer

The mental layer is the third subtle energy body in the auric field. It extends up to 8 inches away from the physical body. The mental layer directly connects to your solar plexus chakra, which is also the third chakra in the energy system. This auric body represents your cognitive processes, thoughts, and state of mind. It is typically bright yellow and contains everything from your ideas, beliefs, logical processes, and intellect to your consciousness. This is where you rationalize your thoughts and ideas. Mental health problems often appear here before they materialize in the ethereal or physical body. When trying to read this level of the aura, pay close attention to the head, neck, and shoulders because these are where it radiates and shines the most.

Astral Layer

You may also refer to this as the *bridge* or the astral body. The astral layer is the fourth auric layer, and it extends up to 12 inches from the physical body. It is connected to the heart chakra, so it contains information about your sense of love, joy, and other high vibrational emotions. It is called the bridge because it links the physical realm and the spiritual realm. To visit the spiritual plane, you must shed your physical body for your astral body. The astral layer often reflects a pinkish color. It is made stronger by loving and intimate relationships with those around you. You can also access the state of your chakras via this body. If you learn astral projection, you can explore anywhere in the universe in your astral form. More importantly, healing takes place more quickly in the astral realm.

Etheric Template

The etheric template is your fifth auric layer, and it connects to your throat chakra. It is about 3 feet from your body. It is responsible for sound, communication, vibration, and creativity. It is called the etheric template because it is the carbon copy of your physical body in the spiritual realm. The etheric template is the blueprint through which your physical body manifested. It often appears like the negative of a photo, but it may vary in color. Everything you create on the physical plane is recorded in the etheric template. This includes your personality, identity, and overall energy.

The Celestial Layer

The celestial body is the sixth subtle energy body, and it is connected to the third eye chakra. It is the representation of your subconscious. It is the point where your consciousness comes to connect with your spiritual mind. When you meditate and do other spiritual practices, this is the place that your consciousness comes to. The celestial body contains information about dreams, memories, spiritual awareness, intuition, trust, and unconditional love. You can only have an experience greater than yourself by tuning in with it. This layer carries a powerful vibration, meaning that your frequency vibration must be on a very high level to tune into the celestial body. With a strong celestial body, you have the power to communicate with spirits and receive psychic messages.

The Ketheric Template

This is the farthest away from the physical body but is the closest to the spiritual realm. The Ketheric template is the seventh and final subtle energy body in the auric field. It is connected to the Crown chakra. There, you can find information about all your past lifetimes. You can also become one with the universe in the Ketheric template. This auric body vibrates at a frequency higher than all other layers. It is the shield of all the other auric bodies and is the home of all knowledge and possibilities. It contains a blueprint of your spiritual path in life, detailing every event you have experienced over your lifetimes. It is your link to the Divine, Source, Creator, All That Is, God, or whatever you believe in. The higher your spiritual body, the closer the Ketheric template is to your physical body.

Many people believe there are other layers of the energy field that are yet to be discovered. Until they are discovered, though, these are the ones you need to know and learn how to read.

How to See Auras

Seeing auras is easy if you are clairvoyant. But clairvoyants cannot see it. To read your aura or that of another person, you have first to know what the auric field contains, i.e., its seven layers. Now that you know that, the next step is to learn how to see it. You must start practice with yourself before you move on to other energetic objects. If your dominant psychic sense isn't clairvoyance, you may not see the aura, but you can sense or feel it. And if you have multiple dominant psychic abilities, that means you can see, feel, or sense the aura, which is good for you. To diversify your options, below are different exercises to "see" the aura through different psychic senses.

Exercise 1: Feel the Aura

If you are a kinesthetic person, it is easier to feel the aura than read it. In psychic terms, being kinesthetic means being clairsentient. As defined previously, clairsentience is the extrasensory perception of feeling. It allows you to feel and perceive things beyond the material plane. Your hands are the most vital tools you need to feel the human energy field and the subtle energy bodies. To perform this exercise, you need to find a quiet space far away from distractions and interruptions.

- Sit in your usual meditative pose. Close your eyes and find your breath. Connect with it and notice it enter your body, move through it, and exit the body. For some moments, this is all on which you should focus.

- With your eyes still unopened, firmly rub your palms together for 30 seconds. Make it as brisk as possible.

- Stretch your hands out in front of you. Note that your elbows are slightly bent, and your palms face each other about a foot apart.

- Slowly, draw the hands together. Don't let them touch.

- Again, repeat the step above as slowly as possible. As you repeat the movement, notice the sensation in the space between your hands. Repeat and repeat the action.

- As you do this, don't open your eyes, or stop breathing in and out gently. If you disconnect from your breath, reconnect again by observing its entry, movement, and exit from your body. This will help stabilize and ground you.

- Pay attention to space between your hands and notice any sensations, thoughts, and images that appear in your mind as you repeat. Be conscious of what is happening between your hands.

There is no right or wrong way to do this exercise. What you are feeling in that moment is yours, so own it. You are experiencing your perception of the energy bodies of your aura. With practice, the feeling you get from auras will become stronger and more dominant.

Exercise 2: See the Aura

For seeing auras, practice makes perfect. Work on seeing your aura first before you practice with other people. Once you see your own, that means you are ready to see other people's auras. Initially, you will find you can only see the lower levels of your aura. With consistency and practice, you can eventually see the higher levels of the aura. As always, find a quiet and dark place for this exercise. If you can't find a dark spot, wait until dusk to practice this technique. I think you should allocate a part of your house specifically for meditative sessions and exercises like this. That way, you don't have to find a new spot every time you want to practice. Plus, if you keep practicing in one location, your senses become acclimated to the environment, heightening your memory and focus.

- Sit facing a white wall with your feet firmly on the ground. Use a chair to support your back.

- Connect with your breath and do a quick breathing exercise to put yourself in a relaxed mode.

- Stretch out one of your arms toward the white wall. Let your palm face the wall while you bring your fingers to closer together. Gently reduce the intensity of your gaze and let it become softer. Maintain a soft gaze as you look at your hand. You should start to see the outline of your aura around your hand.

- Spread your fingers apart slowly while you hold the soft gaze. Focus on the space between your fingers and notice what is there.

- Over time, you will start seeing the outline of your aura around your hand and fingers. Initially, the field may be colorless. But with time, you will start seeing the different colors surrounding it.

- Immerse yourself in the moment and patiently observe your hands and fingers.

As you practice more regularly, you can do this exercise during daylight or other light conditions. After a while, you won't even need the white background to see your aura. You can use a white sheet of paper to create a backdrop if you wish.

Exercise 3: See others' Aura

You can practice with a partner if you have consistently seen your aura without a white background.

- Ask your partner to stand against the white wall in your practice room. They should stand a couple of inches away so they don't touch the white background.

- Stand a few feet away from the partner so you can see their full shape, from head to toe. Make sure you can see the white wall behind them as well.

- Plant your feet firmly on the ground and do a quick breathing exercise.

- Close your eyes for a moment, then open them. With a soft gaze, appraise the other person's whole body. Notice anything that raises on the white wall. Do not be eager to see something. Just observe them gently.

- Soon, you will see the aura rising around their head and upper body. This is the easiest part of the aura to see. It will initially look colorless, but after a few consistent practices, the color will appear.

Seeing auras requires you to be dedicated and patient. With time, you will become a maestro that won't even need an exercise to see the auric field. Don't stop practicing until you get to that point.

What is next after seeing the aura? Reading them.

Aura Colors and Their Meanings

The colors of the aura, their hues, tone, intensity, and sharpness reveal plenty of information about your physical, emotional, mental, and spiritual wellbeing. Here, I explain the meaning of aura colors.

You may define color as a wave journeying through space. Depending on the distance between electromagnetic waves' peaks, your eyes register varying colors on the energy spectrum. In other words, your brain interprets the spaces between electromagnetic waves into colors. Your aura shows different colors because its energy bodies all vibrate at different frequencies. The frequencies and waves are what you see as colors when you see the auric field. Reading the aura is all about interpreting the colors that appear when you see the energy field. Below is a brief and detailed insight into the colors of the auric field and their meanings.

Red

As you already know, red is the root chakra's color. Often, when red appears on a person's aura, it is tied one way or another to their root chakra's functions. This color appears in varying shades in the auric field. Sometimes it is deep, other times, it is as clear as day. Another shade is almost muddy, whereas some appear excruciatingly bright. Each shade of red that appears in the aura has different meanings.

Red typically appear in the auras of brave and fearless people who are grounded in the earth. People like this naturally understand their physical reality and this allows them to embrace the material world's desires. If you have red in your auric field, it means that you are passionate, adventurous, dynamic, and unapologetic. You don't fear mortality, sensuality, over-indulgence, and other adrenaline-triggering activities. Dark, muddy red usually connotes that an individual is saddled with negative emotions and past trauma. It may also represent exhaustion, low energy, or over-working.

Orange

This color appears in the field of people who place much value on their relationships and interactions with others. Orange emits joyful and positive vibes. It often relates to positive energy about money, time, energy, love, resources, and work. If you have orange in your subtle bodies, it means you love teamwork due to your sociable and relatable personality. You are also highly perceptive and dynamic. You are quick to establish friendships with people you have just met because you are good at it. Orange also means you love adventure. You are interested in everything the world offers you, which makes you a thrill-seeker. Because you crave newness and adventure, you may become addicted to relationships or find it difficult to commit to a single relationship.

Yellow

Yellow in your aura indicates that you have a strong sense of self, confidence, and the ability to inspire feelings of greatness in those around you. Yellow resonates with strong vibrations, which usually stem from happiness. As someone with yellow in their energy field, you are a natural leader. You know how to take charge and lead the pack. You also have an incredibly high energy level, which means you don't tire of leading or positively motivating other people.

Individuals with yellow auras are naturally full of joy, generous, and attractive to other people. However, dark yellow holds a negative connotation. When the yellow is a dark shade and is dense, it suggests that you are battling self-criticism, self-doubt, overconfidence, or perfectionism. You are primarily operating from your ego-driven self.

Green

Green in your auric body means you radiate and glow with unconditional love. Whenever you come into people's presence, they feel your life force energy because its magnetic pull is super strong. You may be drawn to animals and nature. You are also inclined to be a natural healer. When someone comes into your presence, they instantly become peaceful and relaxed. That is how powerful green is. In the entire auric color spectrum, green is one of the most balanced colors. That means that people with green auras are also very balanced people. If the green is dark or murky, it could be a sign you are harboring feelings of envy and jealousy in your energy field.

Blue

Blue indicates a person with impeccable communication skills. If you have blue in your aura, it means you can speak your truth and express yourself; there are no limitations. With blue in the energy field, you have a strong ability to communicate clearly with others.

The lighter the shade of blue in your aura, the more positive and peaceful your energy is.

Indigo

Indigo is typically found in intuitive and sensitive people. Indigo in your aura means you are perceptive. Strong intuitive abilities let you know things before they even happen. You are empathetic in a way that goes beyond the usual empathy. By nature, you are a seeker, and you perceive the world as something bigger than yourself. You live life by going with the natural flow of things. Suppose the indigo in your aura is murky. In that case, it could mean you are disconnected from your intuitive self, and you struggle with self-doubt and uncertainty.

Violet

This is the same thing as purple. A violet auric field means you are idealistic with a vision for your future. You can see the bigger picture while noting the smaller details. You have a high degree of originality, which makes you innovative, progressive, and open-minded to anything that involves the universal matrix.

Other colors of the aura include:

- Pink
- Magenta
- White
- Turquoise
- Tan

Although the ones I explained above are the main colors that appear in most people's auras, some of these may also appear as the main color in a person's aura.

Chapter Nine: Daily Exercises and Habits for Strengthening Intuition and Psychic Ability

As you continue your psychic development, keep an open mind. Most importantly, set no expectations. If you have expectations and fall short, it can set you back a couple of years. Keeping an open mind allows you to immerse yourself fully into any psychic experience you have. Rather than anxiously anticipating when you will have a psychic or intuitive "hit", you will be focused in that moment and won't even realize until a hit comes to you.

If you cannot let things happen in their own time, you likely won't make a great psychic. The key is for you to "get out of the way," doing this allows your clair senses to take charge of your perceptions and your experiences. Be ready to let go of yourself and just surrender to your psychic senses.

You can do certain things every day to strengthen your intuition and become more advanced every step of the way. Meditation is one thing I typically recommend to new psychics. Not only will meditation help you gain an insight into your baseline, but it is also crucial to find your quiet place. In this context, the quiet place refers to your

Ketheric template, where your consciousness goes when you are in a meditative session. This is the place where you can become one with your mind, body, and your psychic senses. You probably won't get it right on your first try, but you can reach that state quickly if you keep practicing.

As you go by your day, make passive observation a habit. It is key to clairvoyance. The psychic senses point is for you to pick up on what other people don't pick up on. Don't put your ego in charge as you strengthen your psychic ability. Don't judge yourself. Don't criticize. Don't stress. If you have a friend who is also practicing psychic development but seems more advanced than you, don't judge yourself. Suppose you express any negative emotion in a scenario like that. In that case, it means that your ego-self is driving you. Instead of concerning yourself with anybody else's progress, focus on yourself. Open yourself up to the sensations in your body. Observe the words that go through your mind and the imagery that often arises. Doing all the above makes it easy for you to recognize when you receive a psychic message.

Find a journal where you record your daily experience with psychic trails. Record the trails and tests. When you fail, write down why you think you failed. And when you get it right, write down whatever you think is the reason. At any time, you can look back on the information you write down in your journal to find a pattern or assess your growth.

Since you will also have more vivid dreams and nightmares once you start psychic development, write the dreams down. Sometimes, messages come from the third eye through these vivid dreams. If you don't write down your dreams, you may find it hard to establish a recurring pattern in your dream themes. Keeping a journal is very helpful because it is a way for you to give yourself feedback and evaluate your spiritual growth. You can never go wrong if you give yourself feedback based on your performance and development.

When you just start psychic development, it is always very exciting. But it is easy to lose the excitement and enthusiasm if you don't find a way to incorporate practice exercises into your routine every day. Also, this is the kind of thing you may not want to learn with people around. The process itself is already vulnerable, but when you add people who don't understand the mix, it could become hard for you. The key is to find a way to handle yourself without worrying about judgments from people around you. So, how do you get enough daily practice with no one giving you the side-eye?

Well, I have three clairvoyant and psychic exercises for you. They are easy to try for yourself, so you won't need a partner. And don't forget to record your experiences from this exercise.

- **Exercise 1: Guess the Next Song:** This is a great and fun exercise to help you practice your psychic ability when alone in the car with your radio. I like this exercise because you can do it even when you are not in your car. If you have the music player or radio on and your earbuds plugged in, you are good to go. While you are listening to a song on the radio, Apple Music, Spotify, or any of your music apps, let your mind wander away mid-song. Then, right before the next song, bring your mind back and try to guess the next song's title before it comes on. You may hear the beginning of the song start to play in the back of your mind.

- **Exercise 2: Jeopardy:** Although this exercise is called jeopardy, it is a fun exercise. It may even blow your mind. This exercise is fast-paced, meaning you can't mull over your answers. When asked a question, you immediately say the first thing that comes to your mind. You will give a lot of interesting answers. Sometimes, you may recall how and why you know the answer. At other times, you don't know why or how you know the answer. Suppose your psychic development has kicked off. There, you will find yourself saying a lot of "How did I know that?" when doing the jeopardy exercise. The important thing is to be mindful of how you received the answer. Think back and see if it was due to an experience you have already had or something new. Whatever it is, don't forget to write it down.

If you have a friend who is willing to help you practice, below is one psychic exercise you can do with them.

• **Telemetry:** If your friend has a family heirloom or any other thing like that which doesn't belong to them, you can use it for telemetry practice. Make sure your friends know who the owner of the item is/was. The item could be anything from a watch to a picture or an old coin. Use the object to meditate and write down your feelings during the meditative session. Then, tell your friend what you saw and confirm some of the information with them.

The exercises above are easy to integrate into a daily routine, so don't fret about missing out. If you are consistent with the practice every day, they will even become a habit quickly. Don't forget your daily meditation and affirmation, and dietary changes. These things may appear little individually, but together, they can make a great change in your life.

Conclusion

Clairvoyance may be an inherent ability, but you need practice and consistency to use that ability. Psychic development can be a long and slow process. Be sure that your head is in the right space before you begin the awakening. Importantly, do not open the third eye unless you are sure that you can deal with the consequences. As you progress in your psychic awakening journey, do not be afraid to seek guidance from those who have already had the experience before you. It can be a great help. Finally, let go of the ego before you begin!

Here's another book by Mari Silva that you might like

MARI SILVA

HIGHLY SENSITIVE PEOPLE

The Hidden Power of a Person Who Feels Things More Deeply and What an HSP Can Do to Blossom

References

Are Auras Real? 15 FAQs About Color, Meaning, More. (2018, December 3). Healthline. https://www.healthline.com/health/what-is-an-aura

Are you Psychic? 7 Psychic Abilities You Might Have. (2020, October 21). The Carousel. https://thecarousel.com/wellness/psychic/

Clairvoyance | History of ideas and intellectual history. (n.d.). Cambridge University Press. Retrieved from https://www.cambridge.org/nz/academic/subjects/history/history-ideas-and-intellectual-history/clairvoyance?format=PB

Deb, S. (2020, April 22). *Energy Reading Study Guide | How to Read Energy | TheMindFool.* TheMindFool - Perfect Medium for Self-Development & Mental Health. Explorer of Lifestyle Choices & Seeker of the Spiritual Journey. https://themindfool.com/energy-reading/

How To Clear and Remove a Psychic Blockage. (n.d.). Soul Truth Gateway. Retrieved from https://soultruthgateway.com/blog/how-to-clear-and-remove-a-psychic-blockage

Out-of-Body Experiences: The Psychology of Seeing Auras. (n.d.). Psychology Today. Retrieved from https://www.psychologytoday.com/nz/blog/ten-zen-questions/201907/out-body-experiences-the-psychology-seeing-auras

[PDF] PSYCHIC PROTECTION AND ENERGY CLEARING - Free Download PDF. (n.d.). Silo.Tips. Retrieved from https://silo.tips/download/psychic-protection-and-energy-clearing

Signs Your Third Eye Is Starting To See. (n.d.). Holy City Sinner. Retrieved from https://www.holycitysinner.com/2020/01/22/signs-your-third-eye-is-starting-to-see/

The Human Aura Manual compiled by Dr Gaynor du Perez. (n.d.). http://www.study365.co.uk/wp-content/uploads/2018/08/Module-13-The-Aura.pdf

Third Eye Chakra Healing For Beginners: How To Open Your Third Eye. (2017, October 19). The Law Of Attraction. https://www.thelawofattraction.com/third-eye-chakra-healing/

Writer, C. (2014, January 30). *SENSING ENERGY: 5 strategies to read people's emotional energy.* The Mindful Word. https://www.themindfulword.org/2014/sensing-emotional-energy

Printed in Great Britain
by Amazon